Foundations

OTHER BOOKS BY EILEEN CADDY

The Dawn of Change
God Spoke to Me
Flight Into Freedom
Footprints on the Path
The Living Word
Opening Doors Within

Foundations

of a Spiritual Community

Eileen Caddy

edited and compiled by
Roy McVicar

Findhorn Press

Set in Cygnet on Macintosh SE
Design and layout by Philip Mielewczyk, Bay Area Graphics
Cover illustration © Lawry Gold
Printed and bound by Billings & Sons, Worcester, UK
Published by Findhorn Press, The Park, Findhorn,
Forres IV36 0TZ, Moray, Scotland

Printed on recycled paper

CONTENTS

We would like to make it clear that the 'Findhorn Community' referred to in this book is not the local Scottish village of Findhorn but the community that has grown up around the Findhorn Foundation.

INTRODUCTION TO THE SECOND EDITION

Eileen and Peter Caddy were still recovering from the shock of suddenly losing their job running a luxury hotel when, in November 1962, they towed their caravan onto a rather unprepossessing caravan site at Findhorn beside the Moray Firth in northern Scotland. Here they set up home with their three young sons and a friend, Dorothy Maclean, who lived in a small extension to the caravan.

Today that same caravan park is the home of a large, internationally-renowned spiritual community recognised as one of the more stable elements of today's new age movement. The Findhorn Foundation attracts thousands of visitors each year, some of whom stay on or return to join the two-hundred-strong membership. The community runs educational programmes and workshops throughout the year and acts as a centre of demonstration of a new approach to living.

The story of what happened in the intervening years is a fascinating one that has been well documented in various books including *The Findhorn Garden*, by the Findhorn Community, and, more recently, *The Findhorn Community*, by Carol Riddell. The three adults in the founding group had already had several years of spiritual training and experience, but at Findhorn there awaited them a work of a magnitude that even they could not imagine. Eileen had for several years received guidance from her inner voice—her 'God within'—and to her amazement the instructions she now began to get told her that the six people crammed into a tiny caravan and living on National Assistance would grow into a large and flourishing centre attracting people from all over the world.

Although the Findhorn Foundation originally gained attention for its work in contacting and cooperating with devas—the intelligences behind the outward forms of nature—another side of its work has always been the acknowledgement of the innate ability of each individual to make direct contact with our divine essence and to apply it in everyday life. This aspect was embodied by Eileen and Dorothy from the beginning and the guidance Eileen received by making this contact in meditation was instrumental in shaping the community during its early years. The fact that the Findhorn Foundation has survived so successfully for much longer than most similar experiments is with no doubt due to the firm foundations laid by the spiritual work and inner discipline of the original group.

As we move through the 90s the wisdom contained in this book is as relevant now as it was for Eileen, Peter and Dorothy in the early days. Their spiritual lessons have also had to be learned by members and visitors over the years to enable both themselves and the Foundation to grow.

It is still possible to see the guidance working itself out, twenty or thirty years after it was received. One message stated: "I want you to see this centre of light as an ever-growing cell of light. It started as a family group; it is now a community; it will grow into a village, then into a town, and finally into a vast city of light." Although for a long time the community was a fairly defined entity with a specific number of members, in recent years more and more individuals attracted by the spiritual work of the Findhorn Foundation are choosing to settle in the surrounding area to contribute to the centre's growth and a large number of independent projects and business ventures are springing up which are attempting to embody the spirit of the Foundation in their everyday activities.

As the editor of this book, the late Roy McVicar, wrote in his introduction to the first edition, *Foundations* is published not that others should try to follow it like a textbook, but that it may inspire in them the faith and the vision they need for themselves. Even more, he added, the aim is that it may lead others to turn within and find for themselves the only true source of all faith, all inspiration, all love, and from that attunement have a vision of their own part in the overall divine plan.

NOTE
The passages of guidance in this book are presented in two different forms. Eileen's 'voice' seemed to put straightforward directions on how to do something in simple prose form. But when speaking about a spiritual truth, it seemed naturally to do so with a certain rhythmic quality and it is here put in a poetic form.

The editor's narrative appears in a smaller font size than the messages.

Chapter I

SANCTUARY

I was very aware of the Christ presence,
and of a stillness,
of peace and harmony, perfect harmony.
I was then shown a rainbow
which seemed to start from the centre
of the sanctuary.
It stretched right across the British Isles
and out of it came other rainbows,
rather like the spokes of an umbrella,
until the whole country seemed to be
covered with these rainbows.

To understand the supreme and unique place of the sanctuary in the Findhorn Community we have to go back many years to the transforming experience which Eileen had in Glastonbury. There in the silence of a small chapel she heard for the first time the inner voice which was to be the directing power of her life. It spoke the words which from then on were the key to her spiritual development:

Be still and know that I am God.

In that experience, for the first time in her life, Eileen found God. From that moment listening in silence for that voice became the focus of her dedication. What she heard that voice saying day by day gave practical guidance for her life and Peter's.

As she was told some years later:

Electricity has always been there
But until people became aware of it
And harnessed it
It was non-existent as far as they were concerned.
Now it is used all the time.

I am there.
I have been there since the beginning
But until people seek
And discover Me and My power
I am as nothing to them.

At Glastonbury Eileen discovered God and his power. From then on God became the very centre of her life, and her sanctuary was wherever she could be still and be aware of the One whom she learned to love and, because she loved, to obey.

As she listened every day to what this God within would say, she had many lessons to learn. She had to learn what communion with God meant, and what was involved in putting him first in all things. These and other lessons in spiritual living she now shares with all

3

who would experience the same oneness with God and so find the
inner sanctuary of the heart in the depths of their own being.

One lesson is the daily discipline of the quiet time with God:

It does not really matter how late it is
Or even how tired you are.
What does matter
Is that you are willing to do only My will.
Sometimes it is a very good thing for you
To give yourself a lesson on discipline.
Even if it is a great effort to come to Me
And seek My word last thing at night
Do it
Because it really costs you something to do it.

Coming to Me
Just when it suits you
When it costs you nothing
Is not always what is best for you.

When you have to make that extra effort
When you have to seek My help to be able to do it
It brings us so much closer together.
That very closeness is so necessary.

If it means waking up that bit earlier in the morning
Or sitting up that bit later at night
That small sacrifice is good for you.
If you are doing My will no harm can come of it.
It does not mean you will feel extra tired
Staying up late.
When you are willing to forget the self
And put Me first in all things
That is what really counts.

— Living this life
Is not just a case of doing it spasmodically
Or just when you feel like it.
— It means living it all the time.
Only in this way can I work through you
And use you as My channel.

Part of the discipline was to start each day alone with God:

I want you to start the day by finding Me
Right there
In the very centre of your being
Knowing and feeling My peace that passes
   all understanding
Right there within your heart.

If you can do this on waking
You will find a new peace and serenity
For the rest of the day.
Often you are wakened suddenly
And your immediate reaction is to feel resentful.
I do want you to try to be different.
To want to be different
With all your heart and soul
Will bring it about.

Keep on and on longing for it
Seeking My help
Really strive as you have never striven before
And it will come about.
You must believe you can be entirely different
And you will be.

*   *   *

I expect you to keep in touch with Me all the time
When you have 'off times'
It is so difficult for Me
To make contact with you straight away
Like switching on an electric light
For that is the way you should always be
Ready to hear My voice instantly.

It is so important that you learn to do this now
Because when I have something very urgent
   to say to you
You will not have time to say,
'Wait a minute, I must get into tune.'
— You must be in tune with Me twenty-four hours a day.

The way you start the day helps a great deal.
That is why spending your first waking hours with Me
In My presence
Listening to Me
In the stillness of the early morning
Can be the most refreshing and invigorating
   thing possible.
In this way
You are starting on the right foot.

Think on these things
Do not just do them automatically
But wake up with joy in your heart
And run to Me like a happy child
With the deep desire to be with Me
To listen to Me
To talk to Me
To seek My answer to all your problems
Knowing that I will heal all your hurts
That I will bind up all your wounds.

In the comfort of My loving arms
Safe and secure
Start the day afresh
Strengthened and assured of My love at all times.
Give all of yourself to Me
And know that all is very well.

*   *   *

When you listen to My voice
It is the most natural thing in the world to you
It has become as natural to you as breathing
There is no strain about it whatsoever.
This is the way I want it to be.

It should never be necessary for you
To come into a special state
Before you can hear My voice.
You should be able to hear it at all times
In all places
No matter what is happening all around
No matter what state you may be in.

Your need for Me is constant.
As it was in the beginning
When humans walked and talked with Me
So it is happening now.
This is the most wonderful relationship
Any soul could ask for
And this I want you to have.
This is the relationship I long to have
With all My children.
Only the lower self prevents this from happening.

Before coming to the caravan park at Findhorn and in the early years there Peter and Eileen had no clear vision of why they had been guided to that unlikely spot. They were told clearly that it was all part of the divine plan, but it was not easy to see any pattern in what was happening. One of the hardest lessons was to be willing to obey the guidance step by step without being able to see any reason or design in it.

But it was just this quality of spirit which made it possible for the Findhorn Foundation to be built, and this is why sanctuary—the place where all may turn within for their own guidance—is central.

Be very still
Listen to that still, small voice at all times.
That is the voice to trust
That is the voice to believe
That is the voice to obey
For that is My voice.

At times there will be a clamour of voices around you
And you could so easily become confused
    and go off beam
If you listened to all of them.
But you can so easily shut them all out now
And listen to that one voice.
It is like a note
The one true note for you.
You can hear that note at all times.
No matter what is going on around you
You can hold that true note
Sounding it louder and louder
Until all other notes have been eliminated
And that note sounds as pure and clear as a bell.
That is the note you work from
No other.

*   *   *

All you have to do is be ever conscious of Me
And listen to that still small voice which
    comes from Me.
This is the most wonderful relationship
Anyone can have with Me.
Lift up your heart in deep deep gratitude
For you have truly found the way.

Always go with My guidance   *arbeit*
Never against it.
It is when you go against it that trouble starts.
That is why it is just as well every now and again
To read what guidance I have given you
To see if you have carried it out.
If you have not done so
You can then do something about it.

It is not much use if I ask you to do something
And you fail to do it.
I am very patient and loving
And keep on and on showing you the way
But it is up to you to take it.
I can only show you.
The action must be yours.

You know I always want the perfect for you
And that can only be brought about
By your obedience to My word.
When you are all doing My will
There is no conflict.
When there is conflict
Stop
Seek Me
Find out what My will is
And let this apply to everything.

You are not living as individuals but as a group
You can only find perfect unity if you seek My will.

By hearing and following the divine voice one finds the divine plan
for one's life and is thus able to make a unique contribution to the
good of the whole. Only in this way do we know fulfilment and inner
peace which lasts.

How often have you heard or said to yourself
That the proof of the pudding is in the eating.
So with My word!
The proof of it is in the way it works.

Through thick and thin
Through rough and smooth
Through hard times and easy times
My voice has guided and directed you.
You have lived by it and by it alone
It is your whole life
You know now you could live no other way.

All of this is absolute proof to you
That when you put your life in My hands
And your greatest desire is to do My will
Things work out perfectly.
It is not always the way you expect
But you know that I know what is best for you
And you are willing to accept whatever My will is.

There is a clear pattern running through your life.
You may not always be able to see it
Or the working of it at the time
But when you look back
You can see why it has happened.
You can see that if it had not happened

You would never have advanced as a group
You would not have been able to move into the new
As you have.

*   *   *

As long as you obey My word
And carry it out the way I have asked you to
I can really work wonders.
That is when all the forces are going in one direction
And the power is so tremendous
That nothing can stand in its way.

If you follow My guidance in a half-hearted way
Or not fully believing that much will spring from it
The forces are then diffused.
It is much more difficult for Me to carry out My plan.
When you simply fail to carry out My guidance
Or forget to do so
It is just as if My hands were tied behind My back.
I am unable to do anything.

Every lesson Eileen was given had the one aim—of drawing her into an ever-deepening experience of God, of his love and power—the experience which was to be known later as 'attunement'. This experience of oneness with the divine extended into the whole of life, so that people were to learn to live in the awareness of their essential unity with all life—with each other, with their environment, with their Source.

What a truly wonderful gift it is
To be able to tune in to Me any time of the day or night.
That is what is beginning to happen to you.
You are slowly beginning to realise how
    very close we are.

Consider always the wonder of this gift
The glory of this relationship.
That is the only thing that really matters in life,
This relationship with Me.
Once you recognise this
You stop searching and searching for the truth
For you know that you have found the truth.
That all you have to do now
Is concentrate on that relationship
And out of that will spring all else.

Before finding Me
People spend many lifetimes searching for the truth.
They try many devious ways of reaching it
And yet how few have really found Me
Within the centre of their very being.
They found it too difficult to think of Me
Creator of all things
As within themselves.
Yet here I am
And all people have to do is to seek and they will find.
But they seek in every place but the right place
Within themselves.
I am so near that they do not recognise Me.

*   *   *

Keep on affirming that you are one
With the only power in the universe
And you know that I am that power.
Come closer, come closer
And understand with your heart all
    those wonderful truths.
I want you to know and feel My oneness with you
As you have never done before.

Keep affirming that 'we are one'
Until it becomes a part of you.
I am perfect
And as we are one, you are perfect.
Have no doubt about it.
I am love
We are one, therefore you are love.
I am truth
Therefore you are truth.
I am power
You are power.

Let your soul sink right into this truth
That we are one.
Keep on and on affirming it.
Repeat it
Until you know it with your whole heart
Until nothing can make you doubt it.
This deep knowledge
That you are no longer apart from Me
But you are a part of Me
Will enable you to do anything.

*   *   *

Breathe in the breath of life
And as you do so consciously
You are ever aware of Me.
You breathe all the time
But you are not conscious of what you are doing.
It is an automatic action.
Every now and again you take a deeper breath
Which really fills your whole being
And you suddenly become aware of the breath of life
Being drawn into your very being

13

Infilling you.
You then become aware of Me.

Keep ever conscious of each breath you breathe
And you will be ever aware of Me.
As you make contact with Me at this time
It is like switching on an electric light.
When you awoke this morning very early
You found your light on and burning.
You could not remember switching it on
It was simply there shining brightly.

So it should be all the time with your contact with Me
Never should there be this switching off
And switching on
We should be in contact all the time.
The light should be burning brightly all day and night
So there is no division of light and dark in your living
All should be light
All the time.

Realise how much of your time is spent with Me
And how much is spent without Me.
And when you see how many times during the day
You switch off and on that contact with Me
You will be surprised.

*   *   *

You breathe all the time for breathing is life.
You are kept alive because of your breathing.
You know that if you stopped breathing
Life would no longer flow through you.
So with Me, with My presence.
It is always there like breathing

But you take Me for granted so often
And forget My very existence.
This is what the majority of people do.
They are completely unaware of Me.

You have become aware of Me
You know the wonder of being at one with Me
You are indeed mightily blessed.
Keep this awareness of Me ever before you
Never allow it to fade away into oblivion
Or try to run your life without it.

The inner meaning of sanctuary is that it is not essentially a place,
but rather the experience of the divine voice leading us and enabling
us to know our oneness with the Source of all life. The fact behind
it is that God is within, and the true sanctuary for each one is within.
Therefore each of us must learn to turn within to find our divinity
and to hear our inner guiding word.

Seek within
And you will find the answer to every problem.
There is never any need to search in books for the answer
Or even to seek another soul.
The answer is there
Within yourself
For that is where I am.

So many souls waste time and energy
Seeking the answers everywhere but within themselves.
In fact they spend lifetimes doing this.
Life is not complicated really
It is very simple
It is simplicity itself
But you make it complicated.
When you find life is getting too much for you

And you feel weighed down by it
Stop—
And look at a child.

Life is not complicated for a child.
It lives fully in the moment
Enjoying what it is doing.
It does not really worry about tomorrow
And what it may bring.
Life is good for that child
Life is fun
Life is glorious and exciting.

That is really living as you should live.
I have to keep on reminding you
Of the importance of living this way
Because you are so inclined to forget.
You start worrying about tomorrow or the future.
What a waste of time!

Inner awareness
Inner conviction
Is all you need to act upon.
Never allow yourself to be swayed by the outer.
Inner peace and stillness
And a complete certainty of your convictions
Is essential.

When you place yourself in My hands
To use as I will
You cannot hold a part of yourself back.
I ask for all
Only in this way can I use you as My channel.
I cannot be two parts of you
For we are one.

You have to be aware of that complete oneness
Until you see the two melt into the one
And you know fully the meaning of the words:
'I and My Father are one.'
'I in Him and He in Me.'

*   *   *

Think of yourself as having a spring
Of ever-living everlasting water bubbling up within.
All knowledge
All wisdom
All understanding
All love
Is right there at the source of that spring.
And all that is within is waiting to come out
Is waiting to be manifested
As you recognise it and accept it.

You need no teacher, no guru
All you need is an expansion of consciousness
So that you can accept those wondrous truths
Which are there for everyone to accept
When they are ready to do so.
When they are ready not to take anything to the self
But to give Me the full honour and glory.

The lessons given to Eileen by her inner voice are universal and do
not depend on being in any special place or keeping any special
time or following any special technique of the spiritual life. But as
time passed and the community grew, the need for some definite
place in which they could meet for meditation became clear. At first
they met in their caravan as a family along with Dorothy. In other
words the caravan was their sanctuary.

The atmosphere in this caravan
Is so vitally important for the work
And who creates the atmosphere
But you and Peter?
You have a great responsibility.
If you two are united and working as one
The atmosphere will be spread throughout.

I know you are living in a very confined space
Which makes it so much more difficult
But I have placed you here in this confined space
So that you can all learn to work together
As a group
In perfect harmony.

*   *   *

During this time of intensive training
It is far better for you to avoid the hurly burly of town
And remain as close to the caravan as possible.
When you go out from here
Your vibrations are greatly lowered.
They have then to be heightened again
To enable you to continue the work.

Only when you realise fully
That you are in the right place at the right time
Doing the work that I have chosen for you to do
Will you find complete peace of heart and mind.
This is what I want you to do
And find that peace.

The power in this place is tremendous
And is being constantly increased.
This is something which is simply happening

This is of the Spirit
People have no control over it
This power will spread over a vast area
These changes are coming about all the time.

Be prepared for a great surge forward.
Be prepared for more and more people
Who want to come here
And be in this place.
Many eyes will be opened
And will recognise My glory and My power
And many will walk in My ways.

The most seemingly unlikely people will be drawn here.
Judge no one
But see My hand in everything that is happening.

As it was often difficult for Eileen to find quiet in the caravan she
was guided to go each night to the public toilets to find that peace.
This, as she says, taught her that God is everywhere and that there
is no need for a special place. However as the group's numbers
grew, a special caravan was set aside as a sanctuary. But soon even
that was too small. So there was a real need for a central sanctuary
for the developing community.

The ball has started to roll
And nothing will stop it.
It will gather greater and greater momentum.
The power which has been built up is tremendous
It is invincible.
I gave you a vision of hundreds and
    thousands flocking here
This will come about sooner than you imagine.
Sanctuary is a real need
It will be manifested in true perfection

Let there be real beauty
But true simplicity is essential.
The atmosphere will be more important than anything.
Let it be a place of perfect peace
And stillness.
Silence will build up the right vibrations.

Absolute simplicity and real beauty must be paramount
It will be a place of perfect silence and stillness
The building itself will not be anything spectacular
The outer appearance is not important
What is within will be what really matters
For this place will be the very heart
Of this My holy and blessed place.

Absolute simplicity is essential—
Nothing that will distract from the peace and silence
But all blending in absolute harmony.

It will be the atmosphere not the trappings that matter.
This will be a place of the Spirit
Therefore there must be no pictures of personalities
For all are one in the Spirit.
You will see exactly what I mean
As the whole place comes into being.
Many suggestions will be thrown out
But let all be guided by Me.
As this will be the focal point of this centre
It must be perfect in every detail.

*   *   *

I have said one of the main features will be the silence.
The time is drawing very near when it will be unnecessary
to call out names, power points or magnetic centres, when

all that will be necessary will be deep meditation for each one. Of course My word must be projected upon the ethers but sanctuary is not to be used for talk, discussion, daily news or reading of letters.

It will be unnecessary to have rules and regulations. Each soul will know and feel My presence and will immediately sink into the deep silence which is within each one of you. Allow this to develop quietly and naturally. You will find that it will just happen, just fall into place perfectly.

You know that there are certain places where you would not dream of raising your voice or talking or gossiping. There is something about the atmosphere which calls for silence. So will it be with the sanctuary.

Refuse nothing that people may want to send it, but be very, very guided as to what goes into it. Only the right things are to be used and this will all be made clear at the time. You will see and you will know. Step by step it will unfold.

Let there be much light. Whether natural or artificial it does not matter, but let there be light. The more natural everything is the better because then it will not distract. Heating is essential. Some can rise above cold and heat whereas others have not reached that stage yet. Therefore let it be comfortable so again nothing distracts. Let the seating be comfortable, ventilation adequate, and peace and serenity abide.

This whole thing will bring great unity and harmony amongst you all. You will all be of one accord building My perfect temple to My honour and glory. You will see

My hand in everything, and it will be known for its silence and stillness.

*   *   *

Peter has stated how at this time the first vision Eileen had of a simple cedarwood building had become confused because various mediums and sensitives who came each added their bit as to what it should be like, all with conflicting visions. This brought home to them once again that it must be God and God alone who gives the direction and reveals the way.

As soon as there is absolute unity concerning sanctuary it will be brought about. It is not enough to say that a sanctuary is needed. When I give you a clear vision of it as I have done, that must be held without deviating. Up to now there have been far too many deviations from so many different sources and the perfect picture has become blurred and clouded.

Hold the vision I have given you of that simple cedarwood building. I have shown you where it is to go. It is not to have any extensions. I have stressed simplicity and simple it must be. It will come. It will come. I know all your needs and all your needs will be wonderfully met, and the timing will be perfect. Simply know this and it will help to bring it about more quickly.

The secret of manifesting is to have a very clear picture, to be completely united about it, and know that nothing can stop it coming about because it is all part of My perfect pattern and plan for this magnetic centre.

The sanctuary will be the focal point of the whole community, therefore it must be perfect in every detail.

Again let Me stress the need for simplicity inside as well as outside. Beauty and simplicity. You will know exactly what it is to be like when the time comes. So far I have only shown you the outside, the shell. The rest will come. You have seen so many of My promises brought about already. You will see all of them brought about at the right time.

Great things are coming about. The growth and expansion of this place will be beyond all your expectations. It is an organism, not an organisation; therefore it will grow from a tiny acorn to a mighty oak.

*   *   *

The need for the sanctuary is very important and it will come about at the perfect time. It is right to do something when prompted, but never let there be a sense of rush about it. Let it unfold as everything here is unfolding. I have to work in and through channels, therefore it is necessary to keep wide open and in a listening attitude, so you hear My slightest whisper and act upon it instantly.
It is right that plans should be made of the sanctuary, that you find perfect unity and understanding over it. Step by step the details will fall into place.
It does not matter if the power point is not the central point in the building. As long as it is in the building, that is all that matters. Do not expect the whole plan to be given to you all at once. You will have to go ahead in faith, taking each step as it comes.
As soon as the building is under construction, contact can be made regarding carpeting and furnishing. Very great care must be taken over the choice of these. All that is done must create a great sense of peace and stillness and quietness as well as beauty.

It will all come about much sooner than you think
I am guiding the whole project
And it has My full blessings.
This is a great need
And it is being met.
Leave it in My hands
Just follow out My instructions
Step by step
Watch My wonders unfold in true perfection
See My will being done.

If you find yourself limited in any way, realise that it is simply in your thinking. Expand your thinking and limitations will disappear. I have told you I want only the very best, so aim for the very best.

Keep this very much in mind when you are preparing the sanctuary. I do not want anything second best. See the sanctuary as My holy place and you will find your whole vision for it will expand, and you will see that every detail is perfect. When you find yourselves being economical about something for it, stop and realise that you are doing it all for My honour and glory, therefore only the best will do. This will change your whole outlook and you will realise that nothing is too good for Me.

Let every detail be guided by Me. When in any doubt be very very still and allow Me to reveal the right thing.

Great care is to be taken that the sanctuary is not cluttered up by gifts from people who want to contribute something to it. There will be those who will want to do this, and you will have to decline their kind offers very lovingly and gracefully. Let there be nothing in that place which will distract in any way or which will label you in any way; so that all can enter and become part of the whole instantly.

It will be the vibrations in that place which will strike people more than anything else. So right from the start build in those perfect vibrations so that it becomes a temple of light where all who enter will feel perfect peace and love surrounding them, and stillness will fill their whole being, with nothing to disturb or distract. Peace and stillness.

*   *   *

Why be concerned regarding the form which the sessions are to take when the sanctuary is ready? You will find all this will fall into place quite naturally without any strain for you will find My spirit will guide all that is to take place.

As long as there is a need to call out names they will be called out. As long as there is a need for passing on visions and deep experiences this will happen. When there is a need for deep silence this will just happen; the need will make itself felt and it will come about.

So have no fixed ideas about any set form, for there should never be any set form. Be guided by the Spirit in the moment and the perfect will result and all needs will be met in each individual. Great sensitivity will be needed depending on who is there; that is why I say there should be no set form. There may be times when it will be necessary to read out important things, and this should be done. There must be no rigidity.

What you must watch out for is that there is no idle chatter; that only words of power are spoken there, so that power is not dissipated in any way but is built up to great strength. There must be the sharing of those deep inner experiences and visions, of the bringing down of My heaven upon this earth. This is part of the process of the work that is being done here in this place, but discipline will be needed and control of the spoken word.

So be at perfect peace and watch My plan unfold in true perfection. You will find that those souls who have need to spend time in absolute silence will go into sanctuary from time to time alone and find that silence. The needs in each individual are all quite different, but rest assured all those needs will be met and many really wonderful and amazing things will take place in that holy and dedicated place of light and power.

It will become the heart of this centre and the heart power shall flow forth from it to the four corners of the earth. Many true prayers will be answered and My word shall be manifested in form.

You will find the vibrations will be raised in that place to a great height, which is why the unusual will be able to take place. If you do not understand the meaning of these words now, you will do in the days ahead, for I tell you great wonders are to take place here and nothing can stop them.

*   *   *

Every time you enter My sanctuary, no matter what stage it has reached, take with you love and blessings and deep gratitude for the manifestation of it; for this place will be the focal point for the work. It is of tremendous importance and only the right vibrations should be taken into it. You will find when it has been erected and completed, it will be absolutely perfect in every detail. Step by step you will see this come about. It has My full blessings, therefore only the perfect can come about.

You wondered about the size when you saw it go up. Have absolutely no concern regarding the size. You will find it will be perfect and you will need every inch of that space in the days ahead. In fact you will be mighty glad of it. I am guiding you in all that is happening. I see the whole of the picture, you only see such a small part of it. So be at peace and leave it all in My hands. Know that all will work out perfectly.

*   *   *

The time will come when all those on this caravan site will be of one mind and the whole community will be working for the light and doing My will. Simply accept that this will come about. How this will be is really no concern of yours, but the holding of this vision in your consciousness is. Try to understand that the community will not be closely integrated, that many will live as separate units, but will unite in one mind in the silence and in peace and stillness.

That is why it has been essential for there to be the creating of the sanctuary for a place for many to gather together under one roof in prayer and meditation. There will always be the 'close ones' who will be the very heartbeat of the community.

You will not be able to call it a group because it will be too big. It shall be called a community—a community gathered in My name to do My will.

*   *   *

The sanctuary is now, and shall be, a tremendous power house where power will be generated out to the four corners of the earth.

It will become known all over the world and many will be drawn to it and find great strength and help from the power and radiations which emanate from it.

They will find peace and love, light and wisdom, as well as great joy and happiness from simply being there, and

27

many problems will be solved as they sit in complete silence.

My full blessings are upon My sanctuary. Let it be treated as a sacred and consecrated place, where all may find their true selves, find Me in the midst of them, come to know Me and love Me and do My will.

I want you to place these words of Mine upon the door of My sanctuary:

PEACE BE UNTO ALL WHO ENTER THIS
MY SANCTUARY
MAY MY PEACE DESCEND UPON YOU
MAY MY LOVE INFIL YOU
MAY MY LIGHT GUIDE YOUR EVERY STEP
CAST ALL THE OLD ASIDE
AND BECOME NEW IN MY SPIRIT

Let these words be beautifully inscribed for all to see who enter My holy place.

This is My place and these are My words.

Chapter 2
WORK

I saw someone on a surfboard
carried in to the shore on the crest of a wave.
They were swept right up on to the beach
without any effort whatsoever.
I heard the words:

Do all that has to be done on the crest of a wave
so that everything unfolds in true perfection
and nothing is done with effort.

In November 1962, Peter and Eileen Caddy, following the guidance
of the inner voice, settled with their caravan near the coast of the
Moray Firth. With them were their three young sons and a friend,
Dorothy Maclean.

Little did they know then that they would be there for many years,
that they were to make that wilderness blossom like the rose, and
that they were to be co-founders of a spiritual community which
would one day be known all over the world.

All they knew then was that it was the divine plan for their lives
to be there, and that they had many lessons to learn in preparation
for work which God had for them.

What that work was to be they did not know. If they had known
they might well have hesitated. But in faith they were ready to obey
the guiding voice one step at a time, whatever it said.

I have called you to this very place
So that each one of you might be recharged
  with My spirit.
The work that has to be done
Far exceeds anything you ever imagined.
Work very closely together.
You are a very close-knit group
Each having your special part to play.
So much of the new is opening up for each of you.
Be not afraid
For perfect love casts out all fear.

If you can take one step at a time
It all works out.
This is as it should be.
I want you to know that I have not forsaken you
That I am ever closer to you
That I want things to work out perfectly for you

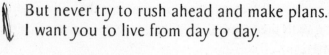

And they will.
But never try to rush ahead and make plans.
I want you to live from day to day.

Never try to look too far ahead
Live in the here and now
Because now is the only time that really matters.
There is so much that you can do—now.
Live one day at a time
And live it well.

The first thing they were told to do was to completely clean the
caravan from top to bottom, inside and out. Peter and Dorothy then
painted the whole caravan so that the light was radiated from within
the very fabric of it. This cleansing reveals a basic principle in
establishing any centre of light: there must be order and cleanliness,
otherwise there will be focal points for the forces of darkness to
become attached and linger.
   This is also a basic principle of spiritual living:

Let there be law and order in your lives
So that you are in rhythm and harmony with
   the whole of life.
There is nothing out of rhythm in nature
All is perfect
All is in order.
It is only people who create chaos and confusion
And as they draw nearer and nearer to Me
And become aware of their oneness with Me
So shall their lives change
And they will no longer be out of rhythm with all life.

When you are in a state of love and light

And you radiate these
Nothing of the darkness can come near you
Or affect you in any way.
Seek always the light.
There is no need to remain in the darkness
Step out of it right now into the glorious light.

The next step was to make a patio outside the front door, with a fence round a small patch of ground where they might grow some radishes and lettuces. For they still thought they would not be there for long. As Peter said: 'If I had been told that we were to have a garden of several acres made out of the sand and gravel, I would have thrown up my hands in horror. Like everything in nature we had to start in a small way.'

So the garden that was to pioneer a new way of working with nature was begun with no clear plan in mind.

The plan you have for the full protection of the caravan is inspired by Me and has My full blessings. Keep that picture of the completed plan in your mind and bring it about. You have the time, but take it steadily and know that every time you put the spade into the soil you are putting in radiations.

Yes, love that vegetable garden. Use all My gifts to the full and be ever grateful for them. Accept all the help that is given you by the family. They too have their part to play. Include them. Let it be a really joyous time for all of you, creating a place of beauty and harmony.

Dorothy Maclean was told in meditation to try to contact the angelic archetypal forces behind nature. This communication with the devic realm added a new dimension to the work in the garden.

The garden is to be a great asset, not a liability. That is why every action must be so closely guided. Dorothy's wonderful contact with the angels of the various plants will make a tremendous difference. She is to have more confidence in her higher self and know that she can do all things. This is a special gift I have bestowed upon her and her alone.

You are working with nature, with the nature spirits and elementals, and are gradually finding harmony with these. What is happening is something completely new because this is the way the new world is to be created. You are all learning the secret of creation in your various ways . . . Work steadily on and know that all is well. Be patient. Things are happening which you are not even aware of yet.

Know that all you are doing in your daily living, whether it is the food you eat, the work you do, the harmony you work in—all are carrying you even further into the new. Let there be no slipping back into the old.

You see how everything is being speeded up. In such a short time the whole development of the garden has come about, and the growth and life force of plants and soil show at what a rate it has been accelerated. So with your own development as a group: each one has shot ahead in a very short space of time.

The garden cannot flourish and flower
Without careful handling.
The garden does not just happen
It has to be worked for
Cared for
Weeded so that it does not become choked

Watered in the dry season.
Plants have to be thinned
The soil has to be cared for.
To get results effort must be made by the gardener.

So with life.
Effort must be made to draw forth the best.
You must make the effort to think right
You must make the effort to unite with your fellows.
Unity does not just happen.
You have to do your part to create unity.

Many many were the lessons they all learned by working together
in the garden. These lessons, as they soon discovered, applied to
all kinds of work and to the whole of life when they sought to live
by spiritual laws. These same lessons are valid now for the whole
community, and have to be learned and followed by all who would
be builders of the new age.

Essentially these lessons involved changes of consciousness. They
can be grouped under three main headings:

The first is the need to be guided in every detail of what one does.
As everything is part of the divine plan, so everyone has their own
unique place in that plan, their own unique contribution to make
to the whole.

At this time
You can learn that priceless lesson
Of living moment by moment under
My minute guidance.
In this way
There need never be a moment of boredom.
Let Me tell you
When to read, when to write

When to walk, when to see people
When to have time with the children.
This is the only way to live a really full life.

You can waste so much time doing the wrong things
If you do not come to Me constantly
To ask Me what I want you to do.
You have no set time for anything
You have no specific job to do
Without My guidance.
You could all either be bored to tears
Or simply go round and round in circles
Doing the wrong things.
Last night you tried to do too many things at one time
With the result you got cross and irritable.
Things did not go smoothly
And by the end of the evening you were exhausted.

It was only nervous exhaustion.
It is well from time to time to see the perfect pattern
Running through all that is happening to all of you.
Always go with the tide
Never try to pull against it.

I want you to realise that the work (on the annexe) must be very guided in every way. This has been given to you all to do for a specific purpose: to teach you first and foremost to seek My guidance over every step, and secondly to learn to work together in perfect harmony.

I want you all to remember this in everything that is done. It is not just a job to be done and completed; it is giving you very important lessons to learn.

Learn to act only on My guidance in everything.
It is so easy
Over the ordinary mundane things in life
Just to go on from one thing to another
Without stopping to find out if you are
   doing the right thing.
You feel that such and such a thing has to be done
And the sooner you get it done the better.
This is an entirely wrong attitude
Because there is a right time for everything
And these times of just being are so very important.

Any people who lack patience and understanding
Let them come to Me
And I will bestow these gifts upon them.
They are so necessary when you are working for Me
When your life is dedicated to My service.

There are times when the wheels move very slowly
So slowly that they seem to be at a standstill.
Impatience floods through you
Your desire is to take things into your own hands
And see some action.

How foolish people are!
Unless work is done at the right time
With My full blessing and cooperation
There is no impetus behind it.
It simply falls on stony ground
And withers and dies.
Be patient
Bide your time until I say go forward.
Then and then only take the action required

Without hesitation
And absolutely fearlessly.
If ever you feel the slightest hesitation
In taking some action
It is better to wait rather than take a false step
And in so doing hold up My work.

Great patience and understanding are necessary
And above all complete obedience to My word.
Do not waste time experimenting
Simply do what I ask of you.
So much precious time is wasted trying
   your own way first
Before doing My will.
Time is getting so short
And there is so much to be accomplished.
The time for experimenting is over.

Find your rightful place in the whole vast plan
And if you find you are not in the front line
Do not let this disturb you.
Remember all sorts are needed to make up the whole.
Simply accept your specific work
Do what you know you have to do wholeheartedly
And allow those who have been placed in the position
Of leadership and responsibility to go ahead.
Give them your full backing and loyalty
They need it and appreciate it.

The second lesson learned in the garden but relevant to all work,
again fundamentally a change of consciousness, is the right attitude
to work. This springs from an awareness of the divine in oneself and
in all things and includes both the spirit in which we do our work

and the standard we seek to attain in all we do, even the most
mundane or seemingly unimportant job.

One of the secrets of building a centre of light
Is concentration
But concentration on a specific object.
To concentrate
On one specific thing at a time
And do that to perfection.

It is so important that whatever is done
Should be done in the right spirit
And in the knowledge that no time is being wasted
If it does take longer than planned.
Time is not the thing that matters
But unity
Cooperation
And really positive thinking are vital.
Whenever there is any negative thinking
It would be far better to sit and do nothing
Until there has been a deep change within.

You now have a purpose in life
Which is more than you could have honestly said
A short time ago.
Be ever thankful for this.
It is a wonderful thing
To realise that you personally are needed
To carry out a work that no one else can do.
You have been trained and tested over years
To enable you to fulfil this work.
It has taken a long time
But now at last you can see the goal in the distance.

WORK

You cannot see the pattern running through your life
But believe Me
There is a very clear pattern running through it.
There are parts of it you would prefer to forget
But you will need this training
To enable you to do what you will have to do.

It is always a good thing to have an aim in life
To know where you are going.
Drifting gets you nowhere.
To know that you are indispensable to Me and My work
Has given you a new purpose in life.
Each one of you has something special
To contribute to the whole.
Let Me use you as I will.
Have no barriers
Remembering that we are one.

✳ I need instruments who are simply instruments
To work through
To bring forth My word without hesitation
And who will act upon it
Because they have implicit faith in My word
And know that when it is acted upon
Things really do begin to happen.

I want to stress with all of you to do the work I have
chosen for you, whatever it may be, wholeheartedly. When
something is done halfheartedly, with lack of faith and
confidence in what you are doing, it has no power. It
therefore cannot be made manifest in form. Only as you
accept your work wholeheartedly can you hope to see
whatever it is brought about.

40

You bring about what you believe—
And only what you believe with your whole heart.
Do whatever has to be done wholeheartedly
Or not at all.
Get into gear
Go full steam ahead
Accepting whatever comes.

Go with it
Accept it
And let there be no pull back.

Whatever job you are doing
See a purpose in it
And learn lessons all the time.

That digging you were doing showed you how important
dogged persistence is in this life. When you tried to shove
your spade into that stony soil, you just hit a stone and
got nowhere. But by steadily loosening the stones you
were really able to make an impression. You need to take
your onward movement in this life more steadily and with
greater persistence. By doing that, anything that stands
in the way will be pushed aside. All this stood out clearly
as you worked, so you were not only doing a job but
learning an important lesson as well.

Perfection is one of the greatest aims
Perfection in all things.
It is one you are ever stumbling over.
You know I want everything done perfectly
Done to My honour and glory

And yet if you can take a short cut
You so often take it.
Short cuts are no good for anyone.
Anything done in a slapdash manner
Is not being done for Me.
It means that the lower self is in control
And not the higher self.
The higher self would not tolerate anything
Done halfheartedly.

You wonder how you can do this
When it is important that you get on with it.
The way you do it
And the attitude with which it is done
Is more important
Than simply getting it done no matter what happens.
It is not easy
But your whole attitude can be changed
In the twinkling of an eye
And you will find that less and less time is wasted
And all will be done perfectly.

Always the higher is striving for perfection.
All you really need to do
Is look and see how you are doing a job
No matter what it is
And if you find you are not doing it with
   your whole heart
Therefore perfectly
It is better to stop doing it until your attitude is right.

my book.   *   *   *

Everything becomes very dull and dreary
When you get into a rut
And do what has to be done automatically
And as a routine.
Every day is new.
That very newness needs to be brought out
    in your living
That is when life can become so exciting and thrilling
Like a mass of beautiful colours
Swirling round
Forming different patterns and designs all the time.
You never know what will come next.
This keeps you alert and on your toes
Because you do not want to miss anything.
All the grey drabness disappears
Life becomes colour
And light
And beauty.

*   *   *

The speeding up process is tremendous.
Come out of your shell all of you
Now is a time of times
Gone are the days of routine
So do not try to step back into them.
Before you is the new, new, new!
Each day will be different
Each day more will be drawn here
None are to be turned away
All are to be welcomed warmly and included.

The third lesson to be learned about work is that it should be done with love. When we are really guided in all we do—doing the right thing at the right time in the right place—then work is truly 'love in action'. It will be done with joy, with a sense of fulfilment, and in harmony with those who are working with us.

I want you to learn to do things
Because you really enjoy doing them
Because you know you are doing them for Me.
Yes, even the most ordinary mundane things
   in daily life.
If only you could remember this at all times
Every deed
Every action
Would take on a new look.
Life would become really exciting
What has always appeared to be a drudge
Would become a joy.

Take as an example the act of polishing a floor.
You can do it positively
So that you can enjoy seeing a lovely shine come up
As you rub
Or you can do it negatively
And just feel it is another job that must be done.

When you start a job
Whatever it may be
See that your attitude towards it is right
And how different it will be.
So with everything in life.
Your attitude makes it one thing or another.
Keep very positive about everything.

There is so much to do
Therefore you are on your toes
Doing what has to be done now
Not concerned about what has to be done in the future.
You know that will open out quite naturally
Like a flower in the sun.
That is the way I want you to live all the time—
Filled with joy and happiness
Doing My will.
Nothing else really matters.
Keep this ever before you
And you can create and draw forth only good.

*   *   *

You attract to you that which you love
Or that which you hate and fear.
When your consciousness is negative
You draw negativity to you like steel to a magnet.
You will find yourself keeping company
With those of like mind
For like attracts like.

When your consciousness is of love
When you are bubbling over with the joys of life
Your heart is filled with gratitude
For everything and everyone.
You will draw to you those happy joyful souls
Who radiate love and joy wherever they go
And your life will be filled with the very best
That life can offer.

*   *   *

WORK

You are beginning to see the importance of working together as a group. It does mean learning to be very sensitive to the other person's needs on the higher levels . . . . This is becoming group conscious. This is the new because it is a case of reaching up and reaching out and feeling deeply the needs of others without any thought for the self.

Teamwork means working together, knowing what the other one is doing and going with them. Living as a group does mean consideration and understanding. No one can live their own life because each life is intertwined with the others. It does not mean that one gets a bright idea and expects all the others to follow. It means each one has to be closely guided by Me.

And you cannot be closely guided unless you constantly seek My guidance.

It must be made clear from the start with all who come here that this is a living, working group, and all must be willing to take part in all that is going on and pull their weight.

The mistakes which have been made in the past must not be allowed to occur again. Those who come must never be under the impression that they are coming for a holiday and will be waited on. They are coming to give and receive on all levels, and this must be clearly understood.

Many hands make light work, and when all are playing their part, it leaves more time for all to really enjoy themselves in so many different ways.

Work is love in action.
So get into action
And work with love

46

And help raise the vibrations of all you undertake.
The more who can do what has to be done
In the right spirit
The quicker will My heaven be brought down on earth.
So start off each day on the right foot
With your heart filled with love and thanksgiving
For everything.

*　　　*　　　*

It takes all sorts to make a world.
I need you all to be different.
Be very loving and very tolerant with each other.
Try to understand one another
And so help to fulfil your individual destinies.

Always try to hold before you the main objective
The goal to be reached:
The bringing down of My kingdom on earth
The creating of perfection in everything
Doing everything with love
To My honour and glory.

Start right now really to love the world you are in
Really enjoy it to the full
It is a wonderful, wonderful world
You are greatly blessed and privileged to
　　be living in it.

The key to the meaning of work in the new age is an awareness of
the divinity in oneself and in all life. It is this which enables one to
follow the lessons which Peter shares from his early training: 'Love
wherever you are, love whatever you are doing, and love whomever

you are with.'

Work is nothing less than the means by which everyone and everything may realise its potential divinity. You take a piece of metal and shape it into a tool with which you can dig the garden, or you prepare food, and you have in that way made it more intelligent. You have raised its consciousness and released its hidden splendour, just as a sculptor makes a rough stone into a thing of beauty.

When you take a dirty floor, scrub it and make it spotlessly clean, and then polish it until it shines, it radiates back to you the love which you poured into it. The divinity of that floor has been drawn forth.

This ability to bring out the inner divinity of things and people is in fact the function of the Christ. David Spangler has said: 'This is why at (the) Findhorn (Foundation) there is such insistence upon perfection in all things, doing all things well, maintaining beauty and order: because it is the Christ's task to uplift all matter and restore it to its own pristine knowledge of its beauty.

'Humans can do this more than any other creature on the earth, for they have the capability of drawing beauty out of nature. When something is made well, when something is cleaned well, when something is planted well, when something is designed well, the Christ lives in it. It has been done with love. We have actually been a link between the life within that thing—whether it is a chair or a dress or a stove or whatever it may be—and the greater life from which it came.

'And by being that link through our love and interest, through our care and concern for perfection, we have infused that matter with life that it knew not that it had. To that degree we have awakened it from slumber. To that degree we also are the Christ.'

I am love
To know Me

You must have love in your heart
For without love you cannot know Me.
Keep the love flowing freely
Learn to love what you are doing
Love your environment
Love all those around you.

*   *   *

It is I who work all things in and through you
When you are willing to surrender your will
And do My will.
That is when the seemingly impossible
    becomes possible
For with Me all things are possible
And all obstacles are swept aside
So that everything runs smoothly
And everything falls into place perfectly.

You behold seeming miracle upon miracle come about.
Learn to live in such a way
That this is taking place all the time
And it becomes your normal way of living.
Expect these wonders and miracles to come about
And you cannot fail to see them happening
    all around you.

There is a time and a season for everything.
It is a question of allowing your life to be
    guided by Me
So that you know the right time and season
With a clear inner knowing
And can move swiftly

49

Following these inner promptings with
   absolute confidence.
It is important
That you really learn to enjoy to the full
Everything you undertake.
When you can do this you will get far more done.
It will be done with love
And therefore it will be done perfectly.
Let perfection be your aim at all times.
When you do something with love
You are doing it for Me.

*   *   *

These principles are true not only for ordinary work but also for
the wider work which was the very reason for the existence of the
community. Every kind of work must therefore be seen in its place
within the overall purpose which the Findhorn Community serves.

There is a vast amount of work to be done
But it will be divided up so well
That the weight will not fall on the few
But on the many
And will become as thistledown.
It will be done with great joy and pleasure
And will be enjoyed by all.

Nothing is to be done halfheartedly.
Wholehearted cooperation is essential
   in all that is done.
Everyone who is drawn here
Will find their own note
And will sound it loud and clear.

Each will have their unique contribution
To make to the whole.

This is a living, working group.
What has been pioneered here
Will be used by many all over the world.
The years of work which have been done very quietly
And steadily
Will bear much fruit.
For all that has been done has been guided by Me
Step by step
And has been done to My honour and glory.
Therefore only the perfect can spring forth.

＊   ＊   ＊

There are as many facets of the work
As there are facets in a diamond.
Everyone is vital and essential
To make up the whole fullness and perfection.
That is why each individual who is drawn here
Has a unique contribution to make to the whole.
You will find no two will be alike
And this is exactly as it should be.

As each soul offers its contribution to the work
You will see the perfect pattern and plan evolve.
Nothing should be held back
Nothing should be clamped down or watered down.

Each soul who comes
May not even be aware of their specific contribution
But gradually it will become evident.

Every gift and every talent must be used to the full
And developed no matter what it may be.

There have been too few workers up to date
And the harvest is great and will become greater
Therefore more workers are needed in the fields
To gather in the harvest.
Let them all come who ask to come
For there is work for all.
The radiations will do the sorting out
You will not have to do anything.

The term 'work' can be greatly misunderstood
For there is inner work to be done as well as outer.
Therefore judge not by the outer eye but by the inner.
Some will appear to do very little on the outer
Yet their contribution may be even more vital
Than that of those who are very active.
Great sensitivity and understanding are so necessary
Plus patience—
Always be very patient.
Some will develop faster than others
Some will need more drawing out and gentle handling.
All will be needed
All will fit in.
The work here will develop by leaps and bounds
Nothing can hold it back now.
So much is waiting to be manifested
These are tremendous days
Days of revelation.
Keep on your toes and miss nothing
Record all that comes for all is vital to the whole.
The place you have reached in your daily living

Has not been reached without effort
Without many vital lessons being learned.
It may all seem so simple to those who come here
And see the way you live.
They do not realise the tremendous work and lessons
Which have had to be learned
To build these rocklike foundations which
   are unshakable.
They do not realise the amazing amount of work
That has gone into the foundations
The corners that have had to be rubbed smooth
The breaking down of the little self
The many ups and downs
And the real pain when there has been any resistance.
It has been a slow business
But those foundations were absolutely essential
Before the building could be started.

Now it all appears to be so simple
A glorious way of life
But it should be made very clear
This has not come about without much hard work
And sacrifice on all your parts
And a complete dedication of your lives to Me
And to My work.
I ask for all
And when all is given
It is returned a thousandfold.
There can be no halfheartedness in this life
It must be complete surrender to Me.
Only then can I work through each of you.

*   *   *

This is a pioneering group
So never look for a blueprint to follow
For you will find none.
Step by step the plan will unfold under My guidance
So never be dismayed or distressed
Never feel lost or uncertain.
My plan is perfect
And only the very best will result. .
What you are doing here many will do
For this is the prototype for group living
In centres of great light and power.

All directives are to come from Me.
Never rush ahead
Without seeking Me first in everything.
Gradually the whole plan will unfold
Be very patient
And never try to force anything.
A flower loses its beauty if the bud is forced open.
Let every petal unfold in its perfect timing
And you have something of true beauty and perfection.

So with this work which you are doing for Me.
What is being pioneered here
Will go out across the face of the globe.
There are times when you are quite blind to this
You get so engrossed in the ordinary things to be done
You fail to see the importance of what is being done
The vastness of it
The true wonder of it.

It is something which has grown from very
    small beginnings

Like a tiny acorn which is planted
And eventually grows to a mighty oak
And its branches will cover the face of the earth.

*   *   *

For all who are in the right place at the right time, who put God
first in everything, all their needs will be met perfectly. The Findhorn
Community was built on this principle of manifestation and is a
visible demonstration of its truth.

I am your source of supply
And all that I have is yours.
My infinite abundance is available to all
But your consciousness must be of abundance
With no thought of lack or shortage in anything.

Feel your consciousness expand
And expand
Let it go on expanding without any limitation
For limitation causes blockages in the constant flow.
With limitation comes fear
And with fear comes stagnation
And when something becomes stagnant
The circulation is cut off
And it goes dead.
Keep the circulation flowing
Let there be a constant giving and receiving on all levels
And know the meaning of infinite abundance.

Know that you are one with Me
That you are one with all the wealth in the world
That everything you have you use for

the good of the whole
That nothing is taken to the self
That nothing is hoarded.
All is there to be used
And to be used wisely.
You are good stewards of all My good and perfect gifts.
You seek My guidance and direction
As to the right use of My infinite supply.

*   *   *

Whatever you undertake to do
Do it with My blessing.
Go into the silence
Feel peace and serenity steal over you and enfold you
And in that state ask and receive My blessing.
Then go forward in absolute faith and confidence
And do what has to be done
Know that I am with you all the way
And that everything will work out perfectly.

The greater the task to be accomplished
The greater your need for My blessing.
Bring Me into every small area of your life
Include Me in more and greater areas
Until eventually you take no step
Without first seeking Me and My full blessing.

All that is undertaken in this centre is done this way.
This is why nothing can possibly go awry
And there is a perfect pattern and plan
    running through all.
You know that all is in My hands

It will work out exactly at the right time
And the right people will be drawn here
To enable it to go forward smoothly
And fall into its rightful place.

*   *   *

Become more and more aware
Of the things that really matter in life
The things that gladden the heart
Refresh the spirit
And lift the consciousness.
The more beauty you absorb
The more beauty you can reflect.
The more love you absorb
The more love you have to give.
The world needs more and more love,
Beauty, harmony and understanding
And you are the ones to give it forth.

Why not open your heart now
And do it?

Chapter 3
PEOPLE

I was shown gathered together in an arena
a great multitude of people of all colours,
classes, creeds and languages.
They were not talking, but just mingling.
There was the most wonderful sense of peace
which seemed to rise from their very hearts
and spread like great rays of light
right across the world.
I heard the words:

It is love that brings peace and unity,
so keep the love flowing
and bring peace and unity to the whole.

A community large or small is made up of people: people who are unique as individuals and have unique gifts to bring to the whole, but who also know how to blend their own uniqueness with that of others in such a way that the good of each is at the same time the good of the whole. It is the very blending with others which results in the fulfilment of each one.

This supreme value of the individual means that people are always more important than any outward form or structure in the community. Even in the early days Eileen was taught by her inner voice to put people first:

The relationship between you and Peter is the key to this place, and creates the right atmosphere. This is not a surface thing but a deep, fundamental one. In future much care and sensitivity are necessary.

This has been a day when you have had to pour out to people, and things have been put into the background. Always try to remember that at all times people must come before things and jobs. You will find, if you put people first and meet their needs, all this will fall into place and the jobs will be done.

You must be prepared for more and more people coming to you. Know always that of yourself you are nothing, but as My channel you are invaluable. Keep yourself very open. Keep ever clear and purified so that you are My channel for My love.

All through the years of building the Findhorn Community, as many came and went, the same emphasis on the importance of people was held.

There is much to be done here
But people must come before all else.

You must never be too busy to give to a soul.
But again guidance is needed over this as well
Because some souls will come to draw.

There must always be a giving and a receiving
For as a soul gives
So will it receive.

There is no mass production in the spiritual life
Each soul has a very special place
Each soul has a very special destiny
Some need help to realise their destiny
Others will plod along
And reach there in the end.

There is no set pattern to follow
Each one is an individual
And should be treated as an individual.

The need of a soul is far, far more important than the housework, washing or anything else. So learn always to put first things first. It is only pride which makes you want to have everything tidy before you allow yourself to sit down. Be absolutely willing to sit in a complete muddle as long as you are doing My will, and know that at the right time all will be straightened up.

These basic principles of the supreme value of the individual and the supreme value of group unity were first learned by Peter and Eileen in the small caravan in which they lived during the early years of the Findhorn Community. In fact it is true to say that they, with their three boys and Dorothy Maclean, formed the first community.

There in a very confined space they had to learn to live and work together in a new way. Sharp personality corners were rubbed off, tolerance and understanding were developed—all the lessons which later on the community had to learn, which are the basis of group consciousness and group unity.

It is important
To keep the atmosphere of the caravan right.
When you are cross or irritable
It shatters the vibrations
Then they all have to be built up again.
That is why perfect peace is necessary.

This does not mean the children have to be quiet
I want them to enjoy themselves
But at the same time they need discipline.

I have told you it would not be easy to achieve unity when you are all in such close contact with each other; but it is absolutely essential that you do achieve it because without it the work cannot progress.

You will find that on higher issues you have found a wonderful unity. But you still have to find it in the small things, and this will not be so easy because the self is very inclined to step in. Just keep on. Try not to argue a point even if you feel you are right and the other is wrong.

If you find it irritates you too much, bring it quickly to Me and let Me give you the answer. Do this rather than even for one second cause disruption and disharmony. Pull yourself up a dozen times a day if necessary, but do it. It will be a complete victory over the powers of darkness when you have accomplished this state of unity amongst you. It can and will be done.

Remember it is My will you all want. Because of that

deep longing in all your hearts you will find perfect unity.
Accept where you are at this time and the conditions you
are living in as part of your intensive training for the days
to come. In this way you will not fight against it but see
it in the right light.

How vitally important
The unity between the three of you is!
This is something to strive for
There is to be no looking into the past
But an acceptance of the absolute *now*
In each one of you.

All of you must be willing
To accept the new from each other—
Yes, complete new teaching at times.
There can be no ruts
As each of you is shown the new.
You will each have something quite different
    shown to you
Pass on that new
Share it with each other.

If there are any doubts
Bring them to Me
I need perfect unity in this group
And perfect unity will be achieved.

This is a time of consolidating
Of blending together and binding together
All of you
Who are so very different
In every way.

It is not always easy
But I never said it would be.
As each of you have your corners rubbed off
And start fitting into My perfect plan
You will be ever grateful.

Living as you are at this time in such close quarters, you each have to learn a greater sensitivity and understanding of each other. You are all completely different. You have each been given different qualities and gifts, and so you cannot be put into a mould. Without understanding there will be constant conflict.

To understand is to stretch your imagination. It is to try to live into the other person's life, and this is a very difficult thing to do because it is so easy to trample and crush if you are not careful and are not very sensitive. This is a deep lesson you all have to learn, and learn as quickly as possible.

What you are learning daily with the children and with each other can and will fan out into a vast work. It has to start here where you are, because unless it starts at the source it will soon become useless.

*   *   *

You must remember that you are pioneers into the new. Problems you have and overcome will not only help you on your way, but will also help many who are learning to live as groups and are advancing into the new.

You are a group and should be able to help each other over these difficulties far quicker as a group than struggling along on your own.

PEOPLE

Never at any time adopt a superior attitude
You are together to help each other
You have not been brought together by your
    own choosing
It is I who brought you together
Placed you here in this specific place
To do a very specific work for Me.
Everything is so carefully planned
Do nothing to upset the perfect planning.

To find perfect harmony among you all
Needs a special effort on all your parts.
It is not just one person's efforts
You are a group
You work as a group
You live as a group
Therefore it needs group effort to attain harmony.
I have brought you together here in this place
To live like this
So that you can achieve this unity
It is up to all of you to do your part
There is so much work waiting to be done
When you are a united group.

*   *   *

These are lessons you all have to learn
Living as a group in very close quarters.
No longer can you live just for the self
Always it has to be for others.

If you each go out of your way to do this
What a difference it will make to the entire atmosphere.

How much quicker the work will go forward.
Every now and again there is a blockage there
Because relationships are strained
Because there is intolerance or criticism within.
It does not always come out into the open
Or even to the surface
And that is worse
Because something that is suppressed
Cannot have the light of truth shone upon it.
It goes on festering
Getting worse and worse.

There must be unity between all of you
And it stems from you and Peter.
Unity does not just drop into your lap
You have to strive for it
To really want it.
It does mean give and take on all sides.

*   *   *

True unity, and true community, is not simply that of workers who
have a common purpose, or even that of a family with the bond of
love. It is that deeper unity which can only come to those who know
that they are one with each other because they are all one with the
Divine. To see the essential divinity in each other is to be one on
the deepest possible level.

You need to learn tolerance
To feel deeply
And above all to love
And that means love with My divine love.
That is what draws together and unites.

I know how little irritations disunite you
Because you are trying to create unity by yourselves
Instead of constantly seeking My help.
You cannot do it
It is impossible
But with My help all things are possible.

*   *   *

Realise that your lives are all interwoven
And no matter how hard you try
You cannot get away from that fact.   *Krие*
It is I who have interwoven your lives in this way
Try to accept it
And not fight to get away.

I want you to aim at perfect harmony in this place
You all need to learn to give and take far more
And a new gentleness and understanding is essential
To bring true happiness and unity to your group.

That will not come easily
Because you are all such individuals
All pulling in different directions.
The only thing
That can possibly make you pull in the right direction
Is allowing Me to guide each one of you.
Constant conflict is exhausting
But when all is in harmony
It is a great uplift.

*   *   *

Be ever conscious of our oneness
And in that state find the oneness with others.
See the very best in them
And draw forth that best
Ignoring all that would disunite
Building always on the positive.

All of this starts within yourself
Find that uniting factor and love within your heart
Impart it to those in closest contact with you
And then to those a little further away.

Then does that love grow
Until your heart has been so enlarged
That it can take on the whole world
And you can feel really at one with the world.
You can do it
And you will do it
But start exactly where you are.

Attunement with the group has its true essence in attunement with God. This reminds us of the place which the sanctuary has in the community as expressing our oneness with each other in the Beloved.

These times of getting together
In the mornings and evenings
Are of vital importance
To the smooth and harmonious running of the whole.
Never feel it is a waste of time
Or that there is far too much to be done.
Learn to drop everything
And come to Me for restoration and unification.

Every moment spent together in My presence
Welds you together
Enables you to go forth
And do what has to be done with new zest
And with love in your hearts
To bring perfection wherever you go
In all you are doing.

These times together are far more important
Than all the work that has to be done
For the work stems from these times.
When you learn to love one another
Learn to seek and find Me
In everything you do however mundane
And do all to My honour and glory.
This is the heartbeat of the whole thing.

Get that right—that relationship with Me
  and with each other
And the whole thing will run on oiled wheels
For the oil of love has been poured forth
And only the perfect can result.

*   *   *

As more and more people came to join the community, the special
gifts they brought needed to be recognised, and each had to be
given the opportunity to develop these gifts to the full.

Every soul who comes here
Brings with them another piece of the jigsaw puzzle
Which has to be fitted into the right place.
There will never be two pieces exactly the same.

my dream at the KKC.

There are times with a jigsaw
When two pieces may look identical in shape
But you find the colour or markings are
    entirely different.
That is why no one who comes here
Has to be neatly pigeon-holed
But allowed to grow and develop
And bring forth these special gifts
That have to be used for the whole.

As each one gives
So will each receive.
It works both ways
There is something for everyone to do
So learn to let go and share your burden.

Every soul who is drawn here
Will have something unique to contribute to the whole.
This is like a wonderful play being enacted:
Each player has his or her part
All the players are not on stage at the same time
But each one comes on to the stage
Contributes their part to the very best of their ability
Then quietly withdraws to let the next take their part.
Some of the parts will be leading parts
Others are just small ones
But all are needed to produce the perfect play.

So work in unison
Entering and doing your part
Then withdrawing quietly into the background
To watch and learn while the others take their part.
There is such perfect rhythm in all this

Just like the seasons of the year
So I say again, go with it all.

*   *   *

Because each person was to develop their own unique qualities,
they had to be given freedom to do so. There had to be no attempt
to enforce conformity.

Each soul must learn to stand on their own feet
And sound their own note loud and clear.
So will be found perfect unity in diversity.
Never try to mould a soul
I alone am the Potter
I alone do the moulding.

Living as a community
It would appear to be easier if all conformed
    to a pattern.
On no account must this occur.
Complete freedom of the spirit is the only answer
In this way
Each one will care enough for the whole
So nothing of the little self enters in.

You are pioneers
There are no charts or maps to follow
Every step that is taken is taken into the new.
Let Me guide you
And mistakes will not occur
And no time will be wasted along the way
And every obstacle will be overcome
With as little delay as possible.

Why are there people?
So you can see yourself.
So you can see Me.

People
People
The world is made up of people.
Open your heart wide
And love people
Bring peace and harmony and understanding
   in the midst of you
Because you are aware that I am in the midst of you.

Try to realise
That group living is the way of life in the new age.
No longer will people be able to live unto themselves
As they move into the new age.
They will realise that they are part of My perfect temple
And have a specific role to play
To enable the whole to function in perfect unison.
Each one has to find what their function is
And they can only do this
By taking time to seek deep within
For that is where they will find the answer.

Stop looking for the problems in group living
Look for the advantages and blessings
Take time to do this
See how much good you can find in this way of life.
You will find
As you start doing this
Concentrating on all the very best
The problems will begin to disappear one by one
You will realise how blessed you really are
To have been brought face to face with this way of life.

To become members of a group

It is important to adjust yourselves
To people and circumstances
You have to learn to love your neighbours
You have to learn to cooperate with them
You have to learn to see yourself as a member
 of a community
As part of a whole
Rather than as a self-important individual.
The little self has to be overcome
To enable you to do this.

When you stop thinking of the self
And start thinking of those around you
And how you can help and serve others
Great changes will take place in your life and living.

*　　　*　　　*

The supreme power which creates true oneness is love. It is this same power which enables each individual to find fulfilment, and to realise all the unique hidden potential within.

Therefore the greatest quality people must develop, if they are to live in a community, is love. By the same token this is the first and the greatest need in the world to bring peace and harmony to all life.

It is love that will overcome the world
It is love that will unite all people
The sooner you release the tremendous power of love
Within each one of you
And allow it to flow freely
The sooner will you see world peace and harmony
And world unity.

When you have love in your heart
All barriers come tumbling down
You behold others with new eyes
You see them as I see My beloved children
Perfect
And you draw the very best out of them
For love sees only the best
And therefore draws forth the best.

*   *   *

The whole world needs love
You need love
Your neighbour needs love
There can never be too much love.
With love comes peace
Unity
Understanding
With love comes universal harmony.

Love those you are with
Love what you are doing
Love your environment
Love those who are your seeming enemies
Love the unlovable as well as the lovable.
When love is guiding and influencing your life
It will be full and abundant and will be fulfilled.

*   *   *

In community new forms and dimensions of relationship must be
explored in many areas of life—friendship, marriage, work. The key
to all is love: love which sees and believes always the best, which

knows and releases the divinity in all life.

I want you to learn to do this.
In every soul you come into contact with
See only the very best
See My image and likeness in that soul
All are made in My image and likeness.

As you learn to do this
You will begin to draw out the perfect in every soul.
There is that perfection in each one
But it has been so covered up *programming*
That it is difficult to find
But it is there
And you can find it as you raise your whole attitude
And see that soul from a completely different angle.

When I speak about love
I speak about the greatest uniting power in the universe
How misused
How trampled on
How misunderstood
Has been that word *love* through the ages.
Now in the new age
It is to find its rightful place
And hand in hand with light and wisdom
Work My wonders and glories.

I need hands and feet and hearts
For My divine love to flow through
Therefore surrender yourself anew to Me each day
So that I can use you in this way
As a channel for My divine love.

By work
By deed
By simple actions
Express My love.
Let it pour forth through everything you do
No matter how mundane it may seemingly be.
The love vibrations need to go into and through
Everything you do.

*   *   *

What does love mean to you?
You hear it
You speak of it
But what does it really mean to you?

It is not a word
It is an essence
It is a power
It is a vibration
It is life.
Love is the most priceless element in all existence
It is a dynamic living force
It is spiritual
Eternal
All-powerful.

Love banishes all evil
Love overcomes all fear
Love is a creative force of unlimited power
Love can restore, rebuild and rectify
Love exalts and glorifies
Love rises above all that would drag it

77

down into the mire.

Love looks deeper than the surface
It looks beyond the visible
Into the innermost depths of a soul.
Love is a balm
That contains the power of healing and renewing
It is a great refiner and beautifier
It is the key to every door.

Love binds
Without love the world would disintegrate.
Love builds the bridge for light to cross
Love is the vehicle of light
Love and light must work hand in hand
One without the other cannot fulfil My laws
In true perfection.

*   *   *

As you open your heart
You begin to understand the true meaning of love
A closed heart knows nothing of love.

True love is never possessive
It never holds another soul in bondage
But longs to see every soul free and unfettered
Finding its rightful place in the perfect scheme of things.
Love is a heavenly gift
It is free for all
Who are ready and willing to accept it.

Love in the true sense is never easy. It goes against many of our natural impulses. Most of us are so selfish and self-centred that we have some hard lessons to learn before we can really love. In this regard, lessons which Eileen thought of as purely personal to herself have now to be learned by those who would be part of a new age community.

Whenever you are at your worst
You can always change very quickly
If you stop thinking about your own condition.
Start thinking about those in desperate need
And then start radiating out to them.
The very act of removing the focus from the self
And on to someone else
The very attempt to feel for someone else
And wanting to help
Changes the whole rhythm.
Next time you find yourself sinking lower and lower
Try this and see what results you get.

*   *   *

You cannot stand back and look on and criticise
And expect to be used to help.
You must know
You must feel
Above all you must love with My divine love
To be able to be used in any way.

It is so much easier
To view it all from a distance
To close your heart so that you do not feel
And you are left unhurt.
But this is not what I require of you.

You have no right to criticise anyone else
Or another's way of life
No matter what it may be.
You may not go with it
But on no account are you to stand aloof
And look down your nose and criticise.

Remember you are no better than anyone else.
If it were not for My infinite love and patience
You would indeed be in the gutter
Living in a hell of your own making.
Spiritual superiority is like a filthy canker
It can rot the soul from within
Not until it is too late does it show itself outwardly.

Humility
And a constant knowledge of My wondrous love
And an everlasting gratitude
Are very necessary
Not just now and again but at all times.
The very act of reaching out to say 'thank you'
The very thought of My love
Brings you immediately into consciousness of Me.

*   *   *

Whenever you find yourself questioning the capability of
loving a very unlovely soul, know that it is with someone
like that that the flow of love needs to be even greater.
All you have to do is to keep yourself clear as a channel
with no limiting thoughts, then I can work My wonders
and bring about My miracles.
The power of love is penetrating. Nothing can resist it

in the end. Just pour it forth unstintingly. You can never give a soul too much of My divine love; it is absorbed like the dew into the flowers and vegetables. When the need is there, so does love meet that need.

You cannot make yourself love anyone
But when you raise your consciousness
You are able to reach that state
When you know that all is of Me
And there is nothing else
No separation
That every soul is of Me
Made in My image and likeness.

Therefore you are one
As long as you remain in that raised state
   of consciousness.
You know the meaning of divine love
And perfect peace and understanding fill
   your whole being.

         *   *   *

Peace, love and harmony
Must flow from the very core of this community
And that starts with the family I have placed
   in your care
And grows out from there to the bigger family
And out and out into the world.
But it has to start from within
And then grow from there.

Never for a moment imagine

You can take the world on your heart
Without starting from right where I have placed you.
Learn to love all those around you
Then work out from there.
When you throw a stone into a pool
The ripples start from where the stone hits the water
And go out and out from there.
Love starts from within a soul
And goes out from that very centre.

Keep ever aware of My presence
Let Me help you over the rough places
Never despair
Never accept failure
Simply know that with My help
You will win through to victory
So take time to listen to Me.

*   *   *

The secret of living in community can be summed up in the word 'oneness'—oneness with people, oneness with all life, oneness with God.

Be one in My spirit.
Oneness cannot be forced
Oneness is not the combining of people's thoughts
And trying to make them live up to some
    prescribed standard
Set by one person.

Oneness comes only when each one is free in spirit
When each one can live their own life

To meet their highest idea
With no one trying to be a reformer or to
   set the standard.

That is being one in My spirit
That is what you feel in the sanctuary as you
   gather each day
That is what you must carry forth into your daily lives.
And live and move and have your being in that oneness.

When each person can truly find that spirit of oneness
Whether it is in a home
A group
A community
A nation
Or a world
Then there will indeed be peace
Peace within
And therefore that peace will be reflected without
And will manifest itself by peace for the whole.

But it has to start somewhere
Therefore let it start within you as the individual
And so grow
From that tiny spark within
To a mighty blaze without.

Chapter 4
OUTREACH

*I saw a seashore with the tide coming in
very quickly, with big waves that rolled
further and further on to the shore.
I heard the words:*

You cannot hold back the incoming tide
So why not flow with it?
You cannot hold back the new age
So why not go with it?
Be part of it
Give eternal thanks for it
That you are consciously aware of it.

The Findhorn Foundation has never been just a community, an alternative to the rat race, a place where one can escape to live in seclusion and peace. It is not an ivory tower, an island cut off from the rest of the world.

On the contrary there has always been in the community a very real caring about the state of the world. Only too well aware of the dangers which are ever present from nuclear conflict or pollution or an energy crisis or the continuing destruction of the planet's skin of fertile soil, the people of the Findhorn Community have always had a keen sense of responsibility to the peoples of the Earth.

In one form or another there has been a deep awareness that what was being worked out quietly and unobtrusively in a corner of north east Scotland was of supreme importance to the whole world.

This could of course be just an inflated ego on the part of those at the Findhorn Community—or it could be a most daring and glorious act of faith, that God had a vast plan for humanity which, if known and followed, could lead to a new age, and that the community was a key point in that plan.

Folly? Delusion? Madness? Or truth? Everyone has the right to their own answer to that question. But Peter and Eileen Caddy were superbly certain that they had been guided to Findhorn as part of that divine plan, that what they did there was nothing less than the unfolding of that plan. And all who are with them share that same daring vision and faith.

Not that the details of the plan were clear at the start. It was only as they took one step at a time and learned the lessons of each step that the way forward became clearer.

From the first days at Findhorn there was a quite definite sense that, although they could not as yet see what it was, there was a purpose for being there, a pattern which would emerge in time.

I want you to know that I have brought you and Peter together for a very, very special purpose. You work as one, and you must realise this fully. How few there are who have been brought together in this way.

It is not by chance
That you have been brought together
Under these circumstances
It is all in My plan.
You have something to accomplish
And it is not impossible.
If you can do it under these conditions
All groups can do it
Therefore never despair
I am with you
And I want you to bring this about.

*　　　*　　　*

You know part of the work that has to be accomplished. I say 'part' because it would not be possible for you to grasp the enormity of it at this stage. You are only a small child learning to walk. You would not tell a small child that it was going to walk hundreds of miles when it can only take a few tottering steps. So with you. It would not help you to allow you even to glimpse the future, for you to see the extent of the work to be done. You would laugh and say it was impossible, or you would become afraid and want to run away.

I just show you a little bit at a time, and with infinite love and patience I help you to take each step forward. The work you have been chosen to do is far too important. I need each of you moving forward all the time—sometimes slowly, then a great surge forward, always towards the goal.

The only thing that matters at this time is the greater work, the work you are doing for Me. All else is as nothing.

The greater work has moved forward
In leaps and bounds.
See all this like the ever moving sea
The waves roll back
But the next wave moves further forward
On and on.
You are just gathering momentum
For the next great surge forward
Know that you are in the right place here.

*　　　*　　　*

Nothing is by chance
There is a perfect pattern and plan
Running through the whole of life
And you are all part of that wholeness
Therefore part of that perfect pattern and plan.

When you see strange things happening in your lives
And wonder why they happen to you
Take time to look for that perfect pattern and plan
And see how it all fits in
And you will see a reason for everything.

In this divine plan it was not by chance that Findhorn was where they came and where they settled. The very place was important, a special place for a special purpose.

It would be best to stay as near Findhorn as possible for the time being. Findhorn radiates great light. It has been prepared over many years.

Sometimes you wonder if it is right to have a long-term policy about this place, especially when you find it hard to see any further than one day at a time.

This place is being very specially prepared for vitally important work. You have been placed here under these circumstances for a very special purpose. There is a truly marvellous thread running through the whole situation.

I want you to look upon this place as a permanent home and know that all the effort that is put into it will bear abundant fruit, not only material but spiritual as well.

Remember this is a vast work. You each have your specific part to play. Therefore you must not hold up the work in any way; but always seek guidance, find what I require of you, and do it wholeheartedly and joyously.

I have told you that there is still work to be done here in this centre—building it up until it is completely protected in every way. The work that is being done by each could only be done in this protected area.

That is why your work is so essential. When that has been completed, then and only then will you be shown what your next part in this vast work is. Things are changing so quickly. It would not be right to give you a further part of this picture. Be content to go ahead step by step.

*   *   *

I never want you to take this centre for granted. It is a living thing. It is growing all the time, growing in strength and power as each of you pours your radiations into it, receiving from above and below further radiations.

So will the power grow ever stronger.

This place is a very important place as a centre. It does not matter where you are to be in the future; this is to be the established centre where much of the work will be accomplished.

Always work with that aim in mind. You will have to work step by step, awaiting developments.

*　　　*　　　*

You are beginning to see the purpose of this place.
When people say without thinking
That this is like a little bit of heaven on earth
That is exactly what it is.
When they say it is like the Garden of Eden
It is just that.
That was where in the beginning
People walked and talked with Me
Where we were perfectly at one.

These souls do not even know why they say these things.
It is because it is what they feel
And they are expressing the truth in their own words.
You will find more and more souls will come like this
And they will come back again and again
Because of this inner feeling.

*　　　*　　　*

By 1965 when the garden was beginning to take shape and a sense of peace and beauty was created by it, the greater purpose began to be clearer and others became aware of its special features.

See this centre in its true perfection

OUTREACH

Filled with souls
Who are here simply to do My will
And to walk in My ways.

This is no dream world
This is reality I am speaking about
This is what you are to hold before you
And so help manifest in form:
Where all your needs are met
Where lack is unknown
Where seemingly insoluble problems are solved
In the twinkling of an eye
Because all any soul wants is to seek My will
And obey it instantly without any thought of self
Because all their faith and trust is completely in Me
And their only desire is to do all to
My honour and glory
Where harmony and peace and deep contentment reign.

*　　　*　　　*

You cannot yet see in what form the work will take up here, but do not let that concern you. Simply let it open up quite naturally and gradually. But realise that everything is being stepped up.

The function of this centre is also changing. There is no longer to be a set pattern to follow, but allow the spirit to guide in the moment. Each soul who comes here will be drawn by invisible threads and their needs will all be entirely different.

This is a living, working centre. Therefore it is necessary for each one who comes to take part in the living and working together. It is most important that they feel part of the whole. There are lessons in this direction which all of you will learn in the days to come.

Resist nothing. Feel a complete welding into a whole in all that takes place. See that every need is met in every soul when they come; all will be different.

Only those who are really seeking the truth will come here, therefore the truth can be given to them straight without anything to veil or disguise it.

Always there must be love flowing out to each and every one who comes, so that they know they are loved and needed, and the very rightness of their being here makes them feel part of the whole.

Love heals all wounds, all misunderstandings, brings harmony where there was discord, joy where there was sorrow, so pour it out unceasingly but very quietly and unobtrusively. Let it seep into everything that is done. It will work wonder upon wonder, and will open up all heart-centres, even those that have been closed for a very long time.

A few drops of the oil of love will work wonders untold.

*   *   *

See the work you are doing as a universal operation
You each have your specific part to play in the whole
You will see that you are all part of the perfect whole
That all you are doing is for Me
And under My direct guidance.

When I tell you
You are to bring down My heaven upon this earth
What does this really mean to you?
It means bringing down perfection,

Beauty
Harmony.

It means learning to live in love and harmony
To love one another
To help one another
And together help raise the vibrations of this earth
To a higher plane of consciousness.
To be able to do this
You must be completely dedicated
To the work I have given you to do
No matter what it is
To accept the fact that I know what is best
    for each of you.

I want you to see this My chosen place, Findhorn
As the headquarters of the vast universal operation;
That here there must always be the nucleus
The very heartbeat of the work.

No matter what coming and going there is
The directives and policies for the whole vast operation
Must come from here through Me.
This direct link with Me is the secret of everything.
Lose that
And you lose everything.
Build on that
And you build on a sure foundation
Immovable and unshakable.

At first the Findhorn Community was seen as a magnetic centre,
with only a small group of people making contact with other groups
all over the world, sending light to them and uniting them, thus

forming a network of light that would cover the whole planet.

This centre is like the heart of the sun
From that heart great rays will radiate out
And touch the ends of the earth.

Faith will move mountains
Know this with all your being
And let nothing stand in the way.
Let My will be done
Let that be your constant prayer
And all else will work together perfectly.

You have much work in radiating light to the magnetic centres. The greater work has begun now. You feel the strengthening and linking of the network of light as you have never done before. Something that has so far only been a picture is becoming very real.

The crooked shall be made straight. See the network of light very clearly. It may be crisscrossed but those beams of light are straight and those radiances can flow to each station in full power. Let this picture grow and grow until it becomes a reality to you.

As you go forth in purest love
And answer the call of many across the ethers
You build the bridge for light to walk upon fearlessly.
Know that when love has built the bridge
The recipient is ready to receive light in all its power.

Love is so gentle
So unobtrusive but so sure
Like a candle it lights the way

It pioneers the way for light.
When you understand the strength and power of light
How very destructive it can be
If it is used wrongly or at the wrong time
You can see the vital role love has to play.
The balance of the two is the perfect combination.

Go forward fearlessly to prepare the way
Sending forth My love radiances.
You will find that it is need that draws forth the love
The greater the need
The greater the love.

*   *   *

Each day as you unite
And send out the light
A very vital work is being done.
Time spent in radiating out is never wasted
Not a second is wasted
Consciously send out light and more light
Love and more love
To individuals, to groups, to nations, to the world.
The need is very, very great
Therefore the need must be answered.

*   *   *

It does not matter what you are doing, you can open
yourselves up and allow yourselves to be used. Simply
become aware of an individual or a group, and channel
light and love towards them. You may be peeling potatoes
or digging in the garden or doing the hundred and one

little things that need to be done, but you can still be used to channel light and love to others at any time.

Remember you are on duty twenty-four hours a day. So be ever on the alert and be very sensitive to the needs of all around you.

Be at peace. Do not strive or strain. All this can come about absolutely naturally. You see a need and answer it. Let your lives be a song of praise, joy, glory and thanksgiving.

*   *   *

As time went on, it became ever clearer to Eileen and Peter that the group at Findhorn did not exist just to do work such as contacting other centres and sending out light to the world. They were in fact the spearhead of a new age. They were pioneering a new way of living which would spread throughout the world and give new hope for the future. People would come from every land to learn this new way and then go back to live it out wherever they might be.

Have I not told you over and over again
You are pioneers of the new
You are a spearhead.
Your way is rough and stony because of this
But it will be easier for those who follow
Because many of the stumbling blocks will be removed
And the pitfalls will be revealed.

The mistakes you have made in the past
Need not be made by others.
You are smoothing the way
So no more time need be wasted.
Everything is being speeded up.

OUTREACH

You often feel that you are on the edge of a volcano
Which is ready to erupt at any moment.
This is indeed the state of the world at this time.

The life you have so taken for granted is unique
Many there will be who will long to live it
Who will be drawn here.
You have started in a small way to do
  a tremendous work
And it will grow and expand very rapidly
Be prepared for this.

        *   *   *

You are indeed pioneers and explorers into the new
The way you are opening up will be used by thousands
And not just by a few.
It is so easy to lose sight of the goal
In your everyday living
And fail to see the unique way in which you are living
Because of the very simplicity of your living.
You fail to see how vitally important it is.
When you are too close to something or somebody
This can happen only too easily
Stand back every now and again
And view it from a distance.

What has begun
Is to go on from strength to strength.
What is happening now is absolutely new
There is no blueprint to follow
No lines to run along.
Think big thoughts

Nothing is fantastic
Nothing is impossible
Absolutely anything can happen now
A tremendous power has been released
And nothing can stop its onrush.

You have all been brought together
So that My spirit can infill you
None of you will ever be the same again
There is no going back from this moment onward
Your lives have become new
Arise and walk in the new.

What you have been pioneering here in this centre will
have to be put into practice and lived in a great many
places. Group living is a thing of the future.

This is a living, working group, and what has been
pioneered here will be used by many all over the world.
The years of work which have been done very quietly and
steadily will bear much fruit, for all that has been done
has been guided step by step by Me, and has been done
to My honour and glory. Therefore only the perfect can
spring forth.

Just a handful of people, guided and directed by Me,
with their lives wholly dedicated to Me and to My service,
can change the old way of life into a completely new way.
This is what you are doing step by step.

All is new
So step out fearlessly into the new
You are pioneers of the new age
Of a new way of life

You are developing a prototype for group
 and community living
You are doing what many long to do
But do not know how to go about it.
How you live
Where you live
Your attitude towards each other
The giving and receiving
The rough edges that have to be rubbed off
Everything you do
Is forming a pattern for this new way of life.

Your way of life is being boldly put on the map
It will be there for all to see
To follow and to learn
All this is in My perfect plan
This is the way it is to come about

Gradually the greatness of the task they had undertaken became clearer to Eileen and Peter and those who were with them. The spiritual community at Findhorn was nothing less than the growing tip of humanity. This was the vision and the faith which inspired and made possible all that was done, and kept them going through the years of preparation.

What has taken place during this time is so tremendous
It has changed the course of history already.
Keep ever alert
You will behold this wondrous truth open up
And grow and develop.
The speed at which this happens will astound you all.
There is not a moment to be lost in freewheeling
Each of you will effortlessly move ahead

Doing what has to be done.

Tremendous things are happening now
Nothing can stop the onrushing tide of light and love
Which is being released.
Every soul must now choose the way
There can be no more sitting on the fence
Every soul will now step one way or the other
Will be carried with the tide of events
There can be no arguing
For the time has come in everyone's life
When they must choose and choose wisely.
Never before has there been such a dividing of the ways.

Very great changes are about to take place
Not just in your life
But in the whole universe.
It will not be a comfortable time
For those who try to go against it
It is terribly important for each one to go with it
With no fear
No concern
Simply knowing that this great upheaval is necessary
This cleansing is essential
Before the next stage can be brought forth.

From this time onward a new phase of the work will begin.
You are wondering what form it will take. It will open up
quite naturally. Just keep yourselves open, so I can use
each and every one of you as My channels to bring forth
and develop this new phase of the greater work.

This will be a great leap forward. Let there be no
resistance. So much is happening on the higher planes

which must now be brought down on to this plane. This
is something which will be happening to many groups,
this new release of power.

*   *   *

The work here will develop by leaps and bounds
Nothing can hold it back now
So much is waiting to be manifested.
These are tremendous days
Days of revelation
Keep on your toes
And miss nothing.

You each will have a tremendous part to play
In the events which are to take place.
Is is I who brought you together
It is I who give My full blessing on each
And weld you into one.
You have been linked down through the ages
But have now been brought together again
At this specific time
For a special work which you will do together
It will unfold so simply and so naturally.

The love between all of you is limitless
And indestructible
This is a magnetic centre
The power is being stepped up all the time
So all who are in tune will be drawn here.

Do not just talk about the new heaven and new earth
It is up to each one of you to bring it down

Into your lives and living
To make it reality.

Do not talk about love and loving
Live it
So that all can see what it really means.

How many times have I told you
That words without action are meaningless and useless.
They are like hot air
That evaporates into nothingness.

You are to bring down My kingdom on earth
By the way you live and behave
So your lives are an example
A joyous example
Which all will want to follow.

*   *   *

Although this work was so great, each one had a part in it, no matter how insignificant that person might seem to be. The divine plan for the whole world meant that there was a plan for each individual. Each one could put God's will first in life and be used as a channel to bring the kingdom of heaven on earth.

You have to accept the fact that you are indispensable to Me, that without you there is a part of the jigsaw that cannot be completed, that you have an important part.

Realise that if you do not have this new faith in yourself you are but a piece of flotsam tossed about by the tide of everyday living. You have nothing to anchor yourself to, and every soul needs an anchor. The tides of life are strong and you could drift aimlessly about. But with this anchor of faith, in the knowledge that I have need of you, you will remain as steady and firm as a rock.

Never sit back
And say the world is in an awful mess
The country is in an awful mess
And there is nothing much you can do
As an individual
To help the whole situation.

With love in your heart
And a complete surrendering of yourself to Me
To use you as I will
I can use you as a channel to do much to help
And to help many souls floundering in the darkness.

When you sit in peace and stillness together each day
You become a tremendous power as the vibrations
   are raised
And you open yourselves up
And allow Me to use you
To channel My divine love and light out into the world
And into the lives of individuals.

*   *   *

In the days ahead
As this centre of light grows and expands
More and more souls will be drawn here
Each one will have something specific to give
To the building up of the whole.
They will have to find out themselves

What they have to contribute
And then give what they have.

You will find
That many new and wonderful gifts and talents
Will come to light
And each one must be used and developed.
This is another way
In which a completely new phase of the work
    will develop.

As souls learn to contribute the gifts they possess
So the community grows and expands.
No one living in the community can live unto themselves
And just take, take, take
And give nothing.
Let Me use each one of you
So that you can give of your very best
In everything you do.

*   *   *

Most souls long for peace and security
But they do not know how to set about creating it.
They do a great deal of talking about it
They know it must be done on a world basis
Or else the world will destroy itself
So they try to do this by repeated conferences.
All this is good
But it is starting at the wrong end
At the top instead of at the foundations
And you cannot build a house of any sort
Without starting at the bottom

With the foundations.

As you think, so you are
As a nation thinks, so it is.
If its outlook is one of aggression and war
It will surely create war
And no amount of talking about peace will bring peace.
When there is greed, hatred and jealousy
At the heart of a nation
No amount of talking about peace will bring peace.

Change the thinking of a nation
And you change its whole outlook.

How can this be done?
It all starts with the individual
It starts from within
First achieve peace within your own self
Within your own home
Within your own community
And you only do this
When you learn to love one another
And live for each other
Instead of for the self.

From that sure and rocklike foundation
You can then go forth
And take peace into the world.

*　　　*　　　*

In order to come through these early years the group required a
strong faith, for there were many difficulties in the way, many things

to discourage them. Only faith in God, in his continuing guidance and blessing, in his limitless resources to meet their every need, could have carried them through.

There is a very special purpose which will be revealed to you as you continue faithfully to do this work. It is not always necessary or right for you to know the reasons for everything. Sometimes it is good for you simply to act in faith, and so build up your faith and strengthen it.

You know how much of this work is based on faith, yet so often your faith begins to waver because you do not see any concrete results. Doubts and fears begin to creep in. How can I unfold My wonders to you if you have not got faith, a really strong unshakable faith?

I have to hold back so much until your faith has been built up, and reveal just the smallest particle of the wonders that are waiting to be revealed to you. The quicker your faith is built up, the quicker the new will appear to you.

Be strong, strong in faith and trust. I would not deceive you. You may be sure there has been a plan running through everything that has happened to you.

*　　　*　　　*

If there is a need
Know that that need is already being met
It is a case of learning to realise
That I already know all of your needs
And that I meet these needs.
But you
With your firm belief
Have to manifest them.

OUTREACH

I have told you
That you are to work miracles in My name
Therefore know that you can do this
And when an opportunity presents itself
Instead of flinging up your hands
And saying you cannot do such and such a thing
Immediately turn to Me
Place yourself in My hands
And say 'use me as your instrument'.
Let go of any strain
Affirm that you can do all things in My name
And simply do them.

*   *   *

I want you to believe in My wonders
Believe in My miracles
As you have never believed before.
I want nothing half-hearted in your belief.
You know the promises I have made to you
Down through the years
Some you have seen come about
Others not yet
But from now on I want you to know
With all your heart
That all I have promised will come about.

Hold on to this
In so doing you will help to bring it about.
I want each of you to face this question
Of believing My word:
You either do
Or you do not.

If you do
Then know that everything I say, I mean
Everything I promise, I will bring about.
When I ask something big of you
I never leave you to do it on your own.
You have to take the initial step
Because that is the one thing I want you to do
But once you have done that
You will have help from every side.

Seek that help
And you will always find it.

*   *   *

To attain anything in life
To learn the laws of manifestation
A soul has to learn the art of concentration
Pinpointed concentration
For without this it cannot be done.
You have to learn patience
Persistence
Perseverance:
To go on and on despite all
Holding the vision of what is to be manifested
And know without a shadow of doubt
That at the right time
It will be brought into form for all to see.

When you have experienced the wonder
    of manifestation
Your faith becomes stronger and stronger
And you know the meaning of the words

'Faith can move mountains'.
The more impossible the situation
The stronger the faith and concentration needed.
All this has to build up gradually
It does not happen overnight.

Never try to do this in your own strength
But keep seeking My guidance and direction
Over every step you take.
The art of manifestation is the way of the new age
This is the way you are to live at all times
And so attain all your needs whatever they are.

Let those needs be for the benefit of the whole
Never for the self
For no good will come of anything manifested for self.

I know all your needs
And will meet them
Even before you are aware of them yourself
When you surrender all to Me
And leave all in My hands.

*   *   *

In obeying the guidance Eileen received, in building the outward structure of the Findhorn Community, and in ever keeping the vision clear of what was to be done, the leadership and drive and dedication of Peter was an absolute essential. Over and over again it was made clear that he had a unique place in this work and that he had gone through a very long training and preparation for it.

Consider the qualities of a rock: it is firm, immovable,

can withstand all the elements without being affected in any way.

Now consider Peter. He is a rock. He has rocklike qualities which are absolutely essential for the tremendous work he has to do. He must know where he is going, and must sweep anything and everything aside which stands in the way.

It is a hardness and ruthlessness which you (Eileen) find hard to understand because it is so opposite to the way you work. I have given you each different qualities which should never be compared.

Suppose Peter was uncertain of himself. Supposing he kept pulling himself up saying he was wrong. Suppose seeds of doubt kept popping up. He would be of no use. I need him absolutely rocklike and immovable for this work that he has to do.

He is a very great leader
This needs to be accepted by you all
He needs the full backing of all of you
This makes things far easier for him
But whether he has the full backing of you all or not
He will not waver in his task
He will bulldoze his way through
To the goal and to victory
With the help and cooperation of each of you
It will speed things up.

*   *   *

What Peter has said about the necessity of getting rid of the old to enable one to build the new is the truth. Peter has a vision of this place, a vision I have given him. That vision he holds before him, and then he starts bringing that vision down onto this level. He knows what he is doing.

Therefore he can be ruthless because he knows that out of that ruthlessness perfection will be forthcoming. If he did not know what he was doing, if his vision was dim, then you might be worried. But this is not so. His vision is crystal clear and he knows what he is doing.

Peter has the qualities
The determination
To see through the most astounding and
    fantastic things.
He has been trained and prepared for this
    through lifetimes
And what he has accomplished in times gone by
He will accomplish again in days to come.

Nothing will daunt him
Nothing will take him off the path he is on
Great will be the success of this vast operation
An immovable rock is needed at a time like this
And in Peter I have that rock.
I can rely on him absolutely
There are very few I can say this about
In absolute confidence
But with him it is so.

Peter is a leader, and one day will become a great leader of many souls. But he has important lessons to learn. A great leader holds the reins, but at the same time draws forth the very best from within each of those he is leading. That best has to be used for the whole work.

You each have such a different role to play. Each one is just as important as the other in your various ways. You are all needed, and greatly needed. But so very often you get the feeling that you are superfluous.

This is wrong. This is why there is often a feeling of imbalance in your group. This has to change. Learn to work together in perfect unison, because everything you are doing you are doing for Me.

It is absolutely essential that Peter holds all the reins and is in control of the whole vast operation. It is a vast operation. You only see a tiny part of it, and so it will be with each of you. Peter sees the whole picture and where he cannot see some aspect of it he will search until he finds it.

He needs help and cooperation, not a constant pullback from each of you. It is the self that rises up and creates opposition. Rid yourself of that self and flow with the tide, doing all to help.

Build and never hinder. Peter has been given a tremendous mission to accomplish, and he will do it no matter what obstacles are thrown in his path.

I have given him this mission
And I am with him in all he is doing
All his inspiration comes from Me.

When he sees a certain action has to be taken
Even against great odds
He will take it despite all opposition.
He will see this mission through
Never, never will he take 'no' for an answer
Great will be the outcome
Great will be the victory.

Simply know that he is doing My will
And do all to help him.

This I say to all of you:
Choose the right path and walk in it
Looking neither to the right nor to the left
Keep your eyes on the goal
You are the spearhead.
The path which Peter is pioneering
Will be followed by thousands and thousands of souls.
This is the new.

'(The) Findhorn (Community) is based on the realisation that the Earth and all humanity are entering a new age.'

—David Spangler

Give thanks that you are here on the Earth at this time. Every group working for the light has a specific work for which it is being prepared.
Therefore it is very necessary that you each seek until you find what work is yours. When you have found it, hold on to the vision I give you of it, and let nothing pull you off or distort that vision.

I want you even now to build for the glorious future, for the new age.

What is being built here at this time is for the future. See it grow and flourish in every way. Be not afraid to expand in every way.

Do it all with complete confidence and faith, for all that is being done has My full blessings. Only the perfect can come out of it all.

Chapter 5
CHANGE

*There was a picture of an ugly duckling
being transformed into a beautiful swan.
I heard the words:*

That divine spark is within every heart
but before the transformation can take
place it has to be fanned, until it is
a flame of deepest love and dedication
to Me and to My service.

The Findhorn Community has been called 'a place of vision'. It has also been called 'a place of demonstration'. It can truly be said to be 'a place of transformation'.

David Spangler said, '(The) Findhorn (Community) is based on the realisation that the earth and all humanity are entering a new age'. The early group at Findhorn were told many times that they were 'explorers and pioneers of the new age'. But what exactly is the new age?

It has been defined in terms of a 'change of consciousness' and it is this which brings home the personal nature of the new age. For such a change of consciousness cannot be organised into existence nor can it be brought about by an act of government. It must be experienced by each person, one by one, and it is this change which the Findhorn Community really exists to bring into being.

Change will be necessary
Therefore do not resist change.
Expansion will be necessary
Therefore do not resist expansion.

Open yourselves up
Allow yourselves to grow and expand and change
Without any effort or resistance.
Those who cannot change
Because they do not want to change
Will simply be left behind.

The precise nature of this change was defined by David Spangler: 'The new age is fundamentally a change of consciousness from one of separation and isolation to one of communion, attunement and wholeness.'

Seek and find your direct link with Me

Retain that link no matter what is going on around you
For it is through that link that all things are possible.

That link with Me, the divine
Is the source of all power
And it is this power which creates miracles
My divine laws made manifest.

What are miracles but My divine laws in operation?
Work with those laws
And anything can happen.

It is identifying yourselves with the oneness of all life
With all wisdom
With all power
That opens the doors
And enables the laws to operate within each one of you.

Why watch miracles happen in the lives of others
When they can just as well happen in yours
When you attune yourselves to this power and oneness
And accept that you can do all things through Me
For I strengthen you and uphold you
And work in and through you.

Of yourselves you are nothing
But with Me you can do all things
You will behold miracle upon miracle come about
In your lives and living.
Keep your consciousness raised
Be willing to accept your true heritage.
Have you not accepted your oneness with Me?
Have you not accepted that I am within you

That you are all wisdom
All power
All love?

All that is within you will be drawn forth
And used for the good of the whole
And the most amazing and wonderful things will
    come about.
What is more
There will be no limitation to what can take place
For I am limitless
And all things are possible where I am.
In that expanded state of consciousness
You are aware of the oneness of all life:
You are at one with each other
You know the meaning of unity and harmony
Everyone is your neighbour
And you love them as you love yourselves.

This is the answer to everything
For when you can do this
There can be no disharmony and disunity
And as more and more souls learn to put
    this into practice
So shall peace and harmony reign in the world.

It all starts with you
Never point your finger at anyone else
But start doing something about it yourselves
And start doing it now.
There is no better time than the present.

*   *   *

Try to see this time as the start of the new
The birth of the new.
And the new can start right here
In your very heart.
You do not have to wait for anyone else to start it
You do not have to look anywhere
Except in your own heart.
It is as simple as that.

*　　　　*　　　　*

Try to think of this life as a great adventure:
You are going to a new country
Where there are new people
With new customs
Who speak a new language
Who live in a new way
And all your old ways
Just do not fit into this adventure.

If you enter into the new in the right spirit
It can be such a joyous adventure
And you will have no regrets.
Put your faith and trust in Me
And step ahead fearlessly.

*　　　　*　　　　*

How much easier it is for a small child
To accept the new
Because it has not yet got itself into a rut
And therefore has nothing of the old to shed
Before accepting the new.

There is great need for you
To become like a simple little child
Yet it is the hardest thing for you to do.

*   *   *

Have you ever watched a snake shed its old skin, leaving it behind complete and empty, and emerge a thing of beauty—new, fresh and shiny?

It matters not if you have not actually witnessed this, but this is what I want you to do with all the old in yourself. I want you to slide out of that old skin inch by inch, leaving it behind to wither away and crumble into nothingness, and to emerge into the new without a shred of the old left.

A snake does not cling on to any of its old skin. When the time comes for it to cast off the old, all of the old goes completely. It has no choice in the matter. This just happens.

Whereas with people, they have been given free will. They can choose whether they shed all the old and emerge into the new as completely new people, or whether they cling on to part of the old. It may be only the tiniest part of the old, but even that tiniest part can mar the new, can act as a break, a stumbling block to the complete advance.

Therefore look within yourself and see if there is anything of the old which you are still clinging on to. If you find there is, immediately cut yourself free of it and emerge into the new, a new being filled with light and love, a radiant being.

You may think that you have cast off all the old, but remember that the old dies hard and it does not just happen. It needs a very determined effort on your part.

But once you have made this really determined effort and have left the old behind forever like the snake, you cannot go back to the old again.

As it has outgrown its old skin, so you have outgrown the old and there is just the glorious new ahead of you, shining in all its beauty and wonder. The snake would not want to return to its old skin; neither would you want to return to the old life. Let it wither and crumble into nothingness.

I want you to witness My wonders in your life and in your living. I want to be able to demonstrate My power within you. This I will do as soon as all of the old has been left behind, and you are wholly in the new.

I can assure you that this will happen. You are making wonderful progress and at times you think you are completely in the new, but there is still that little bit of the old left. Make that extra effort. Work hard and you will get there.

*   *   *

Change can come so quickly
When you are ready and willing to accept change
And stop fighting against it.

All things are made new
When you can see everything through the eyes of love
Every change
Every move
Every test and trial
All is for the very best
All is to help you grow in stature and strength
To help you to get your values right

To take nothing for granted
To change and change quickly
Without any resistance or resentment.

Why not get rid of the old
To make room for the new
Right now?
Far too much time is wasted thinking about it
Immediate action is what is needed
A clean break is so much better than a prolonged one.
Get into action
Do something about it now.

*   *   *

The new age is the age of group awareness, of learning to live and work in the unity of a group. As most people are individualistic and self-centred in their attitude, there must be a radical change in them to enable them to be a real part of a group, part of the whole. This is the change already defined as the change of consciousness from one of isolation and separation to one of communion, attunement and wholeness.

It is I who brought you all together
A lot of self-willed individuals
Full of faults and failings
With absolutely nothing in common.
In fact I have chosen the most difficult
And you are to be welded into a group
Where there is unity, peace and harmony.

Out of the chaos and confusion
Caused by the self-will in each of you

I am teaching you
I am leading you
I am guiding you into My ways
Until eventually each one of you is no longer self-willed
But lives by My will and My will alone.

As you strive to come even closer to Me
You are bound to find unity
For I am the greatest uniting power in the universe.
When you are at one with Me
You are at one with the whole universe.

Let that be your aim
Knowing that all things are possible.
You are to set the lead for many
Pioneering is always difficult
But really worthwhile.
Pioneer for Me
Know that every battle fought and won is for Me
And brings you ever nearer the goal.
You will reach it
Have absolutely no doubt
As a group you have a tremendous work to do for Me.

*   *   *

There is one miracle you do constantly see and wonder
at: that is the way I have been able to cleanse your heart
completely of any hardness or bitterness towards . . . .

*   *   *

From time to time it is as well to review your relationships with those around you—your motives and attitudes. Living as you do at close quarters as a group, the air has to be cleared from time to time. Deep sharing and plain speaking does help to do this.

Never allow resentments to get bottled up, because sooner or later what is inside will ferment and burst forth, causing upheavals and unpleasantness and disunity. Look within before blaming anyone else for anything.

See what you personally can do to right a wrong, and when you see what you can do about it, do it instantly. Do not wait for the other person to make the first move. You may wait around for a long time if you do. But you can do something now.

Have a good spring clean every now and again, so that you can start afresh.

*   *   *

Love overcomes all barriers
When there is love in your heart
Your whole outlook on life changes
What was black changes to purest white.
Love is the solution to all problems and troubles.

Love Me before all else
Then love each other.
The more you love Me
The more you love one another.
Everything works together for good
For those who love Me
And put Me first in everything.

How can you hope for things to go smoothly

When you kick and struggle all the time
And are filled with bitterness and resentment
And can see no good in anything?

Why not start right now
And change your thinking
Replace those thoughts and feelings
Of bitterness and resentment
With love and goodwill?
Take time to be still
So that you can feel My love all around you
Open your eyes
Open your heart
And see Me in everything.

Let go
Be at perfect peace
And absorb My divine love
Become completely saturated with it
Then let it flow forth from you freely.
Freely do I give My love to each and every one of you
Freely let it pour in and through you
Out to those in need.

With love in your heart
Life takes on a different hue
So love, love, love
Take nothing to the self
And change your whole life and outlook.
I am with you.

*   *   *

Learn to think and feel for others
To do to others as you would have them do to you
To understand and enter fully into their lives and hearts
Pouring out love and compassion to them
Banishing all criticism, judgement and condemnation.

It is not easy to turn the other cheek
When someone hits out at you
In either word or deed
The immediate reaction is to hit back.
Those who have not learned to react in the right manner
Who will give as good as they get
And feel justified in doing so
Will wonder why there is so much chaos and confusion
Why people are so full of hatred, bitterness
      and resentment.
They are blind
They cannot see
That until they have learned to change
      their whole thinking
And start right now to love others as themselves
They cannot hope to change what is going on
      in the world.

Love transforms and transmutes all bitterness
      and hatred
Understanding opens up hearts that have been closed
That have remained cold and unresponsive.
Let the oil of love be used lavishly between you
So that all those difficult and stiff places in you
Can be eased and freed
Until there is a wonderful free flow of love and goodwill
Between each and every one of you

And love reigns supreme in your hearts.
Live
And move
And have your being in freedom and in love.

The greater the change in people
The more love and goodwill there is
The quicker will change come in the world
But it starts in you
And you
And you.
The sooner you realise this
And start doing something about it
The sooner will changes take place all around you
And so out and out into the world.
So start doing something about it now.

There is something new unfolding all the time
Feel yourselves stretching and growing
Become aware of all that is going on around you.
Nothing is static
There is constant movement
Constant change
And every change is for the very best.

*   *   *

Many people resist change. Many people resent change. Many people reject the whole idea that we need to change, or even that we can change. Much of this resistance is because they are not honest with themselves about themselves. They do not want to see themselves as they really are, and therefore the first step towards change is 'to see'.

I can accept change.

I know how you feel
When I have to speak to you severely
And pull you up.
Be very grateful that I can do this
That I can bring these shortcomings of yours
To your notice in this way
Because then you can do something about them.

So often there are blind spots in each of you
And it is uncomfortable
To have these blind spots floodlit with My light
It would be so much more comfortable
Just to go on and on
In the same old way
Ignoring your blind spots.

It is because of My great and tender love for you
That I do illumine all those sores
So that they can come into the light
And be healed.

   *   *   *

I am the light of the world.
I am there at all times.
But when people pull down the shutters
Or blindfold themselves
I appear to be no longer there
And they stand in utter darkness.

As they pull the blindfold bit by bit from their eyes
They can once again see the light
But it has to be done gradually

CHANGE

Otherwise it would blind them with its brightness.

People have to choose for themselves
Whether or not they take action
And remove the blindfold.
No one can do this for them.

So often people choose to remain in darkness
Because their faults and failings and weaknesses
Cannot be seen.
Darkness blinds and binds
People are no longer free but in bondage
Even though they imagine it is more
    comfortable that way.

You know what I mean
For when you are in the dark
You want to be left alone
For fear of what the light will reveal.

*   *   *

As more and more are drawn to this centre
There will be many who will want to join you
And learn to live and work as a group.

Much love will be needed
Deep understanding and tolerance
All will be different
All will need special handling and understanding.
Never try to lump people together
Each one is an individual
Who needs very special care

Each one has specific problems
Which need to be sorted out.

Great patience will be called for
It will not be easy
But keep very close to Me
And let Me guide every word and every action.

*   *   *

Think of a treasure which has been lost for hundreds of years in the depths of the ocean. It has been lying there becoming more and more encrusted with barnacles, until its original beauty is completely unrecognisable.

Then it is discovered at last by a treasure hunter, is brought up to the surface and looks utterly worthless. Someone with no knowledge or insight would not even recognise it as a priceless treasure, and might even cast it back into the ocean as rubbish.

But those with knowledge and insight would take time and patience and very carefully chip off all the barnacles. It might take weeks and weeks to reveal even the tiniest part of the treasure, but those who know will allow nothing to deter them until they have cleansed it completely and it lies before them in its true beauty and perfection.

So with a soul. In every soul there is that true perfection. There is that Christ image. There is that spark of God. It may be unrecognisable with all the dirt and filth that covers it; but those who know, who are sensitive, see deep down beyond all the surface confusion to that which is the truth, and with great love and patience and perseverance will slowly remove bit by bit all that is marring the beauty of that soul, until the perfection is beheld and that soul stands forth in its full glory and knows that it is made in My image and likeness, that it is one with Me.

*   *   *

Do not waste time
Trying to overcome your weaknesses and failures
Simply raise your consciousness
Transcend and free your thoughts
From limitation and illusion
Find within the very centre of your being
Wholeness and completeness.

Know the meaning of true freedom.
The knowing of that freedom sets you free
To do My will and walk in My ways.

Cease struggling
Become still
Cease wallowing in your imperfections
Be perfect even as I am perfect
Know that you can reach that state of perfection.
Never accept limitations
Aim high
And you will get there.
It is only your limiting thoughts that hold you back.

*   *   *

Find out what My plan is for you
Then carry it out without hesitation.

Do not let those petty little things in life
Hold you back from advancing along this spiritual path
Those little petty self-indulgences
Which seem so harmless at the time
But which become like silt in a river
Which gradually clogs up the free flow
Until it becomes sluggish and lifeless.

Keep an even flow
So that nothing can stand in the way
And all is washed clear before it has time to clog.

Fill your mind with positive, creative thoughts
Fill your heart with love
Fill your life with light.
Be love
Be light
Be full of wisdom and understanding
All this is yours
When your life is hid in Me
And you learn to do My will
And walk in My ways.

Learn to meet petulance with gentleness
And perverseness with kindness.
Always return good for evil
And overcome anger by love.
Love will overcome all
So fill your hearts so full of love
That you will overcome the world.
Love is the universal solvent
There is no greater power than love.
Love unites

CHANGE

Love sees not evil but only the good
Love sees perfection in everyone and everything
And turns the hardest heart into a loving heart.
Love has to flow in and through individuals
So open your heart
And let it flow through you.

Layer after layer has to be peeled away
Before the heart is laid bare
And can really know and feel love.
As you learn to think for others
As you learn to serve each other
As you learn to forget the self completely in service
So are the layers of the old peeled off one by one.
There are as many layers to be peeled off
As there are on an onion.
But never give up
Never despair
Simply know
That as long as your greatest desire is to know
And to find the true meaning of love
You will do so.

Readiness to change is a major quality in the new age consciousness. Many people are ready for others to change, but not everyone is willing for the effort and cost and discipline of becoming different themselves.

No one can enter the new
Without a real change of heart
And you can only experience a real change of heart
When you choose to do so of your own free will.
No one can make you change

They can only show you the way.
You have to take it
You have to start the wheels turning
And keep them turning.

*   *   **

When souls enter into the rarified atmosphere of this centre, things begin to happen to them and they are never the same again. They may have to go back into the ordinary atmosphere of everyday life when they leave here, and to begin with they may slip back a little, but never can their lives be the same again. In this atmosphere that divine spark in every soul has been fanned, and gradually the spark becomes a flame, and will grow and grow, and become brighter and brighter.

It may be only a slow process with some but nevertheless it will happen. Others will burst into flame and will go forth and great things will happen to them. They will mount the steeps with springing steps and with joy in their hearts. All obstacles will be surmounted. Nothing will stand in the way of their spiritual advancement because they have seen the light and nothing will be able to stop them from reaching the light.

*   *   **

The old must die
So the new may live and increase and multiply.
When a potato is planted
The old potato rots and withers away
So more and more potatoes can be brought forth.
When a grain of corn is planted in the ground

CHANGE

The original seed disappears
So the new can spring forth in greater profusion.
So within a person
The old must be surrendered and die
So the new may spring forth in all its glory.

Therefore never resist change
Accept it as a vitally important process of life.
Never be satisfied to sit around and vegetate
Content with old ways, old forms
There is so much in life waiting for you
When you learn to let go all the old
And move forward into the glorious new.

Never be afraid of the unknown, the unseen
Simply know that as you move forward into it
It is going to be wonderful.
Expect the very best to come out of it
And it will.
Many sit around dreading what tomorrow may bring
Instead of enjoying to the full
What this moment has in store for you.
Cease worrying about the tomorrow
Today is what matters
What you do right now in this moment of time.

If a seed refused to be planted
It would never grow
If you refuse to change
You will wither away and die.
Life is ever changing, ever new
It is so full of joy and excitement
There need never be a dull moment

When you keep in midstream
And go with the flow
And do not get stuck in a little byway
Refusing to move on.
You face life in the right spirit
The spirit of adventure.

        *   *   *

Circumstances keep changing, and this is where you must learn to be absolutely open and flexible and willing to alter course at a moment's notice.

When you are working with Me, rigidity is of no use. A hard, brittle, unpliable piece of clay is of no use in the potter's hands. It could not be moulded into something beautiful.

        *   *   *

Never be afraid of changes
Never be afraid of expansion
Simply let go
And allow it all to happen quite naturally.

Open your eyes
And see the changes that take place in nature
How naturally a flower unfolds without any resistance
How a tree changes from bare branches to green leaves
Grows and stretches its branches up and
   out to its full glory.
Now let each one of you let go
And relax in My divine love
Allow yourselves to grow and expand

Just as naturally as the trees, the flowers
And see what happens.
Wonder upon wonder will take place
Because there is nothing of the self in the way
To stop the growth and expansion.

Be still
And in the silence let Me reveal My will
My divine plan for you.
It is a glorious plan
Simply accept this
But realise that it will be unfolded gradually
Not all at once.
If I were to reveal My plan for you all at once
You would not be able to take it
No matter how wonderful it might be.

Place your lives in My hands
Leave the rest to Me in absolute faith and confidence
Knowing that I alone know what is best for you.
When you allow Me to direct and guide your whole life
Only the very best can come about.
I am with you always
And when I am with you
Everything falls into place perfectly.

*   *   *

One of the oldest truths which is also one of the most relevant to
new age living is: 'As a man thinketh in his heart, so he is.' In modern
language, 'Change your thinking and you change your life'. Eileen
was often given guidance like this:

Life is what you make it. It can be a wonderful, joyous, illumined, glorious time, or it can be just the opposite. It all depends on your attitude and outlook.

This uncomfortable truth, though at the same time a challenging and inspiring truth, was emphasised and repeated through the years.

You are almost at the end of the old year
A year that has brought great changes.
You have each advanced along the spiritual road
Much further than you realise.
If you could each stand back
And view yourselves personally
You would be able to see this clearly.
As it is you are so close to yourselves
That you fail to see the positive
You see only the places where you have failed.

Make your resolution now
To see only the positive
The best
In everybody and in every situation.
Look for the best
And don't be satisfied until you have done so.

By doing this
You will see everything with new eyes
And to see everything with new eyes
Will create the new all around you.
It will be hard work at times
To keep on stretching into that new vista
Leaving the old behind
But you will find

CHANGE

When you do this at every turn
Your whole life will change.

As you think
So you are.

*   *   *

By your thinking and your attitude
You can determine all the conditions of your life.
Therefore let no fear
No worry
No hatred
No jealousy
No sorrow
No grieving
No greed
Enter into the realm of your thoughts
And be so filled with love
Joy, true happiness and freedom.

When your mind is in the right state
So will your body be free of all pains and aches
You will find a new zest in life
And life will take on a new meaning.
Those things which have bound you like chains
And held you down
Can be broken right now
When you really want them to be broken.

But are you sure you are not holding on to them
For some reason or other:
Perhaps to draw attention to yourself

Or for sympathy
Or self-pity?
Look within your heart
Deep within it
And see what the motives are.

Only you and I know your true motives
No one else does
Therefore only you and I together can do something
  about them.

Never at any time feel your situation is hopeless.
When you allow yourself to do this
You are creating limitations.
And always remember I am limitless.
When your faith and trust are in Me
We can do all things together.

*   *   *

This is a time of spiritually consolidating
Of taking time to be still
Of dwelling upon Me and My word.
Use this time which is given to you in the right way
Let every moment of it be guided by Me.

When you take time to be alone with Me
Only the very best can come out of that time
Because when your mind is stayed on Me
You are dwelling on the perfect
You are creating the perfect within you
And nothing negative can enter that secret place.

You have the key
You can enter that place
And lock the door from the inside
And there dwell in perfect peace and stillness.
Then when you have found that glorious state
   of consciousness
Open the door wide
Share it with all you come in contact with
But find it within yourself first.

Waste no time or energy
Dwelling on negative and destructive thoughts
Dwell only on the very best
In everything and everyone around you.
I have reminded you of this so many, many times
You carry it out for a while
Then you forget
And allow in a tiny negative, unloving, critical thought
And before you realise what is happening
You find your vibrations have been lowered
You become depressed and disconsolate
And are no good to anyone
Not even to yourself.

The only answer to this condition
Is immediately to change your thinking
Start here and now looking on the bright side of life
Looking for the very best
Counting your blessings
Appreciating everything
Giving thanks for everything
You will soon find your whole outlook will change
There will no longer be any room for the negative.

What a responsibility you hold in your hands.
It is up to you what you make of your life.
It is up to you whether you make it a tremendous success
Or a complete failure.
It does not depend on your outer circumstances
It all depends on you
On what is going on deep within you
You can put things right
Right now.

You can go into that secret place of the Most High
There you will find the answer
Put the answer into practice
And hey presto
Darkness will be turned into light
Every step you take will be lighted by that inner light
Which nothing outside can extinguish.

                    *   *   *

Be ever aware of the vitality of your thoughts
Keep them ever pure
Loving
Constructive
Positive.
Raise them out of the mire of materialism
Of self-concern
Of self-justification
Into the realms of the spirit
Keep your mind stayed on Me.

                    *   *   *

Negative thinking, thoughts of hatred and resentment, can affect your state of health. Healthy thoughts create a healthy body. With many souls their unhealthy thoughts are so deep down in their subconscious that if it were suggested that their state of health was caused by some deep-seated resentment, hatred or fear, it would be flatly denied. But I tell you this is the cause of so many of those pains and aches. If only they could be faced up to, and something done about them.

You will always find a person with a healthy, positive outlook on life has a healthy body.

*   *   *

this is unconditional love

My love is like the sun
It shines on all alike
For all are one in My sight.

De Mello

It depends on your awareness how much of it you accept
The more open you are
The freer you are
The more aware you are of My glorious love.

Love heals all wounds
Love breaks down all barriers
Love walks and moves freely where angels fear to tread.
I am love
I am within you.
Expand your consciousness
Accept this
And give eternal thanks.

Many changes in our way of living come about spontaneously with spiritual growth. One of the basic laws of the spiritual life is that we must keep growing, moving and reaching forward into the new. This requires the effort on our part to stretch and seek always to realise the full potential of our divine nature.

When you stop stretching upwards
Things get on top of you
And everything becomes stagnant.
This life is a constant stretching process
There should be no sitting still.

It is like the sea
There should always be movement of some sort.
Life is not like a pond or a loch
Because if it were
You would not advance very far.
The sea is always on the move.
When I tell you to be at peace or to be still
This does not mean the stretching process has to stop
In that state of peace and stillness
You can reach up so much further.

In this life
There is always room to stretch and stretch
There is always something new to learn
Some new height to attain
That is what makes this life so exciting and thrilling
Because there is always something new just round
    the corner.

*   *   *

You are an unfolding soul

CHANGE

Feel this process of unfolding all the time.
Whenever you feel you are stuck in a rut
And have stopped unfolding
Take time to find out what has happened
Where you have failed to see something through
Where you have ceased to stretch.
When you have sought and found the cause
Find the answer
And do something about it without delay.

The process of unfolding should be slow and sure
You never see a flower unfold in the sunshine
It happens very gently and slowly bit by bit
It reveals its beauty
Without your even being aware of it doing so
Until eventually you notice it
And marvel at its glory and wonder.
So it will be with you as your soul unfolds
Wonders are hidden away to be developed
    and revealed.

When you take a rosebud
And cut it open down the middle
You will be bitterly disappointed
Because that bud has not had time to develop
    and unfold.
Its colours
Its beauty
Its perfection
Are marred by this sudden harsh treatment.

The same with the soul.
It has to unfold in its own perfect timing

To reveal its true wonder and beauty
A soul must never be pushed and driven
And only given help when it asks for help.

I have never tried to force Myself upon you at any time.
If you wish to go your own way
And live your own life
You can always do so
Without Me browbeating you into walking My way
But you also know
That as soon as you feel the need of Me and My help
And cry out for it
Whether aloud
Or that deep, silent cry within your heart
That reaches Me just as quickly
I am always there
Ready to help you in every way possible.

When you cry out for My help
Do it always with an open heart and mind
With a determination to do whatever I ask you to do.
Obedience is so vitally important
For a soul who seeks My help.
I can only bring about My wonders
When I have implicit obedience.

Seek at all times and you will find.
What you will find
Will always be My perfect answer to your needs.

*   *   *

Change of consciousness is not a purely personal concern. When people change, the community also changes. When people change, the world will change too.

Tread this spiritual path
With peace in your heart towards all
For blessed are the peacemakers.

Only when all people find peace in their hearts
Will there be peace in the world
And all conflict will cease.

Unite in peace and understanding
Start by creating peace within yourself
Then peace amongst yourselves
Then peace with all those you contact in daily life.
From there start radiating peace
And more peace
Do it consciously
Do not be vague about it
Radiate it to the troubled spots in the world
The more of you who do it
The quicker will be the results.

The majority of people long for peace
But many fail to see that peace starts within themselves
That the sooner they sort themselves out
And find peace of heart and mind
The more they can be used to create peace
Until each and every one becomes a peacemaker.

Think peace
Live peace
And so bring peace into the world.

Chapter 6
THE FUTURE

*I was shown a few seeds planted in a vast area
of ground. I thought how lost they looked.
Then I was shown the process of growth, of
flowering and the shedding of the seeds.
This went on until the whole area was covered
with beautiful plants.
  I heard the words:*

Be of good cheer. This is what is happening here
in this place. From very small beginnings a
tremendous work is going out right across the
world. My kingdom is come. My work is being done
on earth as it is in heaven. Rejoice. Rejoice. Rejoice.

THE FUTURE

When Eileen and Peter were guided originally to go with their caravan to the Findhorn Bay Caravan Park, they thought it would be for perhaps a few weeks, at most a few months.

They knew it was part of the divine plan for them to go there—they never imagined it was the divine plan for them to stay there. It was almost the last place they would have chosen to do the work for which they had been brought together.

They did not know then why they had to go there. They could not see into the future beyond that first step. They had lessons to learn there which were essential training for the future, perhaps these three in particular:

To put God and his will first at all times;
To follow the direction of the inner voice step by step;
To have faith that God would meet all their needs.

These lessons were given to Eileen over and over again, until they had learned them not only for themselves but for many who would come to the Findhorn Community through the years that lay ahead.

You cannot see what the future holds for any of you.
It does not really matter one iota
All it would do
If you could see into the future
Would be to give you a sense of security
Your security is in Me
And the only thing that matters is to do My will.

*   *   *

You realise more and more
That the only way to live is from day to day
Planning ahead is for you quite useless.

You cannot plan too far ahead
But as one door opens up
So will the next
Just be willing to take one step at a time.

*   *   *

I know that at times this thought of ceaseless effort makes
you tired and despairing.
   The reason for this is that you are failing to live in the
moment. You keep on looking ahead and thinking how
impossible it all is. There is no need to look ahead. All
I ask of you is to take one step at a time, and while you
are taking that step, enjoy it. Feel the exhilaration of it,
the triumph.
   Every step should be exciting. Life lived as it should be
lived is never dull.

*   *   *

Know that every single thing
That is done under My guidance
Bears fruit in time
Even when the seed appears to have fallen on
   barren soil.

The ground cannot be barren for always
I go ahead to prepare it
Before asking you to sow the seeds.
The seeds may take a long time to germinate
But they should never be touched or interfered with.

Every action should be made only under My guidance
Otherwise impatience may spoil something
Which if left alone would develop perfectly.
Always you have to learn patience over everything
You take a step under My guidance
Then you have to stand back
And await results.

Sometimes the wheels turn very slowly
But know that they are turning.

*   *   *

You will find that every vision I give to Peter
Regarding this place
Will be brought about.
I have to give it to him bit by bit
Simply because of those limiting thoughts
Which can enter into all of you so easily.

You know that there is a vast world
Waiting to be revealed and explored
All it needs is for you to keep open to Me
And obey My word.

*   *   *

On the other hand just a few weeks later Eileen was given this
message for Peter, showing the need for balance between vision and
patience.

Tell Peter not to jump too far ahead. Each small part in
My immense plan will open up little by little. What you

are all doing here is something much bigger than any of you realise.

It is right for Peter to keep his eyes and ears open and his feelers out, but not to try and jump a river before all the little streams have been crossed.

The future involves many souls, and until those souls have been awakened and see where they fit into the plan, the strain falls on all your shoulders and the work is not equally divided up. That is why too much must not be undertaken all at once.

This whole project will unfold. You may rest assured of that.

*   *   *

Various souls will be drawn here
Like steel to a magnet
Keep building
Have faith that all is very, very well
That the wheels do take time to turn.

If there is a need
Know that that need is already being met
It is a case of learning to know
That I already know all of your needs
And I meet your needs
But you
With your firm belief
Have to manifest them.

*   *   *

None of you have any conception of the enormity of the

task ahead of you. It will only be revealed to you piece by piece.

You have had the training, you have the qualities needed for this tremendous task, and you will see it through to final victory. And great will be the rejoicing.

So go ahead step by step, knowing that no matter what happens victory is assured.

*   *   *

Very gradually glimpses of the future were given to Eileen in the silence as she listened to the voice within. The vision of the work the fledgling Findhorn Community was to do began to take shape. But it was still rather vague and uncertain because they were still not ready to accept the immensity of what they had started.

In 1964 Eileen received this down-to-earth direction:

Never limit Me.
I have so much to reveal to each of you
And the only thing that stops it
Is the way you limit Me with your thoughts.

For example, this morning
When Peter's vision began to expand for this place
And he began to see the possibilities
Of extending the area
You allowed yourself to see it for one moment
Then your mind got to work
And began to limit that vision.

Always prepare for the time
When the wheels will be turning at full speed
Now is the time for preparation and consolidating

And of building up this centre.
Everything has to be constructed and manifested
Nothing just happens haphazardly.
Have patience
Know that all is well
That all is flowing in the right direction.

When I require something to be done
I will make it quite clear to you
Then action must be taken immediately
To put whatever it is into gear.

*　　　*　　　*

By 1965 it began to be clear that a new phase was beginning:

I have told you that you will be coming into contact with
more and more souls. The time of seclusion is over.
During these years, when you have been cut off from all
outer contact, you have learned many priceless lessons
which you will now begin to put into practice and
appreciate.

And by 1966 it was made more definite what was to happen there:

Many things will open up
Which have remained closed through the ages
So be prepared for strange and wonderful happenings
Be prepared for tremendous changes here at this centre
Always changes for the very best
An opening up
A rapid expansion.

On no account are you to do anything about it
Simply keep in contact with those I have placed
    on your heart
Feel the expansion all the time
And see it coming about.
This is to be a centre of fully dedicated souls
Only those who are fully dedicated
Will be able to remain in the vibrations.
There has been a new release of power
But it is all controlled and harnessed
So have no concern for that.

Remember you have not chosen this place
I have.
It is necessary for it to be difficult to get at
So only those who are determined to come here
    will do so
All must be wholeheartedly dedicated
There can be none who are halfhearted
My work calls for all.

                    *   *   *

Although they now knew that changes would be coming, they still
had no clear idea of what these changes would be. One thing they
were told: that their numbers would begin to grow, far beyond
anything they had ever imagined or wanted.

Your group is not going to remain as it is
It will grow and grow
Until you have the right number
Then no one will have to do double or treble duty
Each one will work in their own way

That power will be pinpointed
And therefore will be tremendous.

Do you not realise that as a group
You are affecting the lives of thousands?
The way you live
The way you behave
The thoughts you send out
The work you are doing on the inner is very powerful
And cannot remain only on the inner.
Be not afraid because it is a great responsibility
I have laid upon you as a group
Have you not all been prepared for this work
    over the years?
Have I not gently led you to this?
Understand fully the power of the work you
    are doing for Me
And do it joyfully
And you will behold the results.

*   *   *

Let no doubts enter into your thinking
Expand your thinking
This is something which does not come easily to you
You like small things
Now I am asking you to see something big
And expand your consciousness in every direction
To realise that with Me all things are possible
To see a picture of this place
And hold it in your consciousness
And bring it about
Allowing nothing to stand in the way.

Each one of you can do your part
By thinking very positively of this place
Holding the visions I have given you from time to time
Of multitudes being drawn here
Of the whole area expanding.
Hold the blueprint for this place before you
See it step by step grow and develop.

*   *   *

The ball has started to roll
And nothing will stop it
It will gather greater and greater momentum
The power which has been built up is tremendous
And it is invincible.
I have given you a vision
Of hundreds and thousands flocking here
This will come about sooner than you imagine.

*   *   *

You have been given a vision of the expansion and the
growth of this centre. You have been shown one caravan
after another being put into place in various sites.

You know that this will happen, even though you do
not know the mechanics of the whole operation, even
though you do not know who is involved in the operation.

But this does not worry or concern you. You know that
it will come about, and at great speed.

There is tremendous work being done all of the time,
and power is being constantly radiated out from here.
You will realise how great is that magnetic power by the
number of souls who will be drawn here in days to come.

The power of this place is tremendous
And is being constantly increased.
This is something which is simply happening
This is of the spirit
Therefore humans have no control over it.

This power will spread over a vast area
And these changes are coming about all the time.
Be prepared for a great surge forward
Be prepared for more and more people
Who will want to come here
And be in this place.

Many eyes will be opened
And will recognise My glory and My power
And will walk in My ways.
The most seemingly unlikely people will be drawn here
Judge no one
But see My hand in everything that is happening.

*   *   *

The growth of this centre is like the opening up of a beautiful rose. It is so gradual, and yet before you fully realise it that bud which was tightly closed only a short while ago is in full bloom. Yet you have not actually seen the opening up of it.

This whole work is developing and growing far faster than you realise. The ball has started to roll in earnest now, and nothing and no one will be able to stop it.

Let the heartbeat of this centre go steadily on, completely unshakable, the life-blood flowing its steady course through the whole. All is grounded in Me. All is directed and guided by Me. The pattern is perfect and complete on the higher realms and will be brought down here into this centre step by step.

All My promises are coming about.

*   *   *

So by the beginning of 1967 it was becoming very clear to Peter and Eileen that they had indeed started something tremendous, but they still could not see what exactly it was or what it would evolve into. Without knowing any of the details they could now discern several aspects of the centre, features which were to make the Findhorn Community the unique place it is:

(1) It was pioneering a new way of life for the whole world.

(2) It was a place of synthesis and integration where many different people would be able to unite and work together in love and in harmony.

(3) It was a place of change which would keep on growing and developing along the lines of guidance by the divine spirit.

You cannot yet see in what form the work will proceed here but do not let that concern you. Simply let it open up quite naturally and gradually. But realise that everything is being stepped up—not too fast so you will not be overwhelmed.

The function of this centre is also changing. There is no longer to be a set pattern to follow, but allow spirit to guide in the moment. This is a time of great linking up of all those who are working for the light. Everything is being speeded up, and nothing now can hold up the progress of this place and this work, for all is being done to My honour and glory. The results will indeed be far-reaching, and the name of this place will be on the lips of the many.

This is My fortress. The young and the old will be drawn here. All nations, all colours, all creeds shall gather together in perfect peace and harmony in this place, and the light and love shall increase. The glory of My kingdom shall fill the place, and My love shall flow like a swift-flowing river. All shall know it and feel it and give everlasting thanks for it.

*   *   *

Expect the most wonderful and unexpected
   things to happen
See the work expanding
Beyond anything you have ever imagined so far
See it as world-wide
Sweeping across the world like a mighty flame
See the truth burning
Right into the hearts and minds of My children
   everywhere.

As your thinking expands
As you begin to think big thoughts
So you bring them about one by one.

The whole of the work here is to change
To expand
To grow in power and strength
The few will become many
The harvest is ripe
The time for the gathering in is at hand.

There is much work to be done
But there will be many hands to do the work
And it will become light and joyous.
Many will recognise their rightful place
And will simply fit in
All needs shall be met.

From a tiny acorn has grown a mighty oak
The place will become world-renowned
Nothing can stop this happening now.
Nothing shall stand in the way
Of this great spiritual renaissance.

*   *   *

When you behold the birth of a baby, it is difficult to comprehend that it started as a minute cell, to emerge in all its perfection in every detail. So with everything that is happening here. It is growing and developing in true perfection. It cannot be rushed or hurried. It has to unfold like a perfect flower.

*   *   *

By 1968 and 1969 it was very clear that the work which had been set in motion at Findhorn was of greater significance and held greater potential than anyone could foresee. It was not simply that something new had been created, but rather that a creative process had been started which was still going on and was indeed gathering momentum, and no one could say what the next stage was to be in its unfolding. For this was no human affair but could only be explained as the divine plan which was being worked out by the divine power operating through human instruments.

I want you to see this centre of light as an ever-growing cell of light. It started as a family group; it is now a community; it will grow into a village, then into a town, and finally into a vast city of light. It will progress in stages and expand very rapidly. Expand with the expansion. The foundations go very, very deep and are built on rock; therefore it does not matter how fast the growth takes place. It does not matter how great it grows.

Let go of all fear of it getting out of hand. I can assure you it will not. But it will grow and flower and flourish and glorious will be the results for all to see. All will recognise My hand in everything that is taking place. Let everything unfold quite naturally. Make your needs known and every need will be answered. You are advancing rapidly into a new phase of the work, a really wonderful phase.

*   *   *

Changes happen so quickly in the Findhorn Community that it can be said at any time that we are 'advancing into a new phase of the work'. There is always the challenge to 'expand with the expansion', and those who cannot, find it impossible to stay.

It is unimportant to try to see in which specific ways expansion may come: whether it is to be an actual extension of area, or a new aspect of new age living which is to unfold. The essential thing is the special kind of faith held by those in the community and their willingness and ability to move with the changes when they come.

Try to remember that everything you are doing here in this centre is not being done for yourselves but for Me. Of course you will enjoy the fruits of all that is being done because that is the way it works out; but first of all do it all for My sake or because I have asked you to do it. Take nothing to the self.

Then you will know what I mean when I say, 'All that I have is yours.' I work in and through you to bring about My wonders and My miracles. Simply expect them and see them come about. The whole expansion of this centre is a demonstration of My divine laws working out. Call them miracles. Call them what you like. Live and move and have your being in My divine laws and anything can happen.

There are absolutely no limitations, therefore expect these seemingly amazing things to happen all the time. I can do all things in and through those who love Me and obey My word.

*   *   *

It is necessary for this My centre of light
To grow and expand
This is happening at great speed.

Feel yourselves grow and expand with it
Feel the real joy and excitement as this takes place
Feel part of the whole
And so give of your very best to the whole.

It is a wonderful, wonderful life
You are all mightily blessed
And greatly privileged to be alive at this time
Doing what you are doing
Ushering in the glorious new age.